# BRIAN'S LEGACY

# ALSO BY SIEGFRIED OTHMER

*ADD: The 20-Hour Solution*
by Mark Steinberg, PhD & Siegfried Othmer, PhD


**BOOK CHAPTERS (partial list)**
Performance Enhancement Applications of Neurofeedback
Siegfried Othmer and Susan F. Othmer
*Case studies in applied psychophysiology: Neurofeedback and biofeedback treatments for advances in human performance, W. A. Edmonds, & G. Tenenbaum (editors), Wiley-Blackwell, West Sussex, UK, 2011, pp. 17-30.*

Neurofeedback for the Autism Spectrum
Siegfried and Susan F. Othmer
*Cutting-Edge Therapies for Autism, 2011-2012, Ken Siri and Tony Lyons, Editors, Skyhorse Publishing, 2011, pp 262-267*

EEG Neurofeedback Therapy
Siegfried Othmer and Mark Steinberg
*Chapter 19 in Clinical Addiction Psychiatry, D. Brizer and R. Castaneda, editors, Cambridge University Press, pp. 169 - 187*

Efficacy of Neurofeedback for Pain Management
Siegfried Othmer and Susan F. Othmer
*Chapter 50 in Weiner's Pain Management, Seventh Edition: A Practical Guide for Clinicians, edited by Mark V. Boswell and B. Eliot Cole; Taylor and Francis, Boca Raton, Florida, p. 719-739 (2005)*

The Subjective Experience of Neurofeedback
Siegfried Othmer, Vicki Pollock, and Norman Miller
*In "Mind-Altering Drugs, The Science of Subjective Experience," Mitch Earleywine, Oxford University Press, London (2005)*

EEG Biofeedback: Training for AD/HD and Related Disruptive Behavior Disorders
Siegfried Othmer, Susan F. Othmer, and David A. Kaiser
*In Understanding, Diagnosing, and Treating AD/HD in Children and Adolescents, An Integrative Approach, James A. Incorvaia, Bonnie S. Mark-Goldstein, and Donald Tessmer, editors, Aronson Press, Northvale, NJ, pp.235-296 (1999)*

# Brian's LEGACY

by Siegfried Othmer & Brian Othmer

Produced and Printed in the United States
First Printing, 2013
ISBN 978-0-9895432-0-0

Cover & book design by Carree Michel

# TABLE OF CONTENTS

# INTRODUCTION

*Life was beautiful when I was young, until I underwent an evil change in personality and beliefs. The way I perceived the world, and the way I acted had dramatically changed. This whole change did not go unrecognized by me, and no one could understand it better than I. This change affected my life in ways that I hated. I was put to shame so intensely that I considered death as appropriate self-punishment. Instead I submitted myself to isolation as self-punishment. My bad behavior must either be contained by my own activity, or terminated by my death. Life is better than death, I decided, so at whatever expense, LIVE.*

Brian's journal [September 23, 1989]

It was a watershed event in our lives when my wife Sue and I were summoned by school officials from Roscomare Road School to hear a litany of complaints about the behavior of our son Brian. A number of people were in the room, and they each had their issues to report. Brian had been fighting with kids during recess, and a girl's face had been scratched.

"If you agree to get some professional help, we're willing to give Brian more time," the principal said. "For our part, we will assign a special teacher to him." It was clear they considered us, the parents, to be completely at fault. The counselor was to provide Brian with the loving attention that he was obviously not getting at home. We left the meeting with a torrent of emotions: confusion, guilt, shame—and a determination to put things right.

How had we missed the warning signals? Brian's behavior problems were not news to us, but the environment at home was very different from that at school. At home, Brian had an outlet. He could walk the trails and climb the hills around our house. At school, he was trapped, and acted out against the kids around him. We had not been seeing the whole picture. For months his behavioral issues at home had been getting worse, but the litany of offenses laid at our doorstep was of quite another order.

It soon became clear that the counselor's intervention was having no impact, so we were summoned to a second meeting.

"Brian just spat out obscenities at me!" the counselor exclaimed defensively.

"Your son is clearly severely emotionally disturbed."

Brian could no longer remain at the school. We were asked to make other arrangements.

We left the meeting feeling absolutely depleted. Brian reacted with typical insolence and disconnection, which, in our opinion, disguised a world of hurt and confusion. But who could know how he was really feeling? Questions mounted. What do we do now? How do we explain this to Brian? What school will take him? And how can we correct behavioral problems we don't understand?

Like most people in our culture, we firmly believed that a child's behavior was the parent's responsibility. It was our duty to teach Brian to behave. Not only was this not working, but matters were slowly going downhill. They might even be accelerating.

Had we failed our son?

The year was 1977. Brian was eight years old. Professional help for cases like this was rare. Fortunately, our pediatrician understood something we did not: He suspected a neurological involvement, but he was not yet prepared to share that with us until he had more to go on.

"We need to have a look at Brian's EEG," he said, and ordered a clinical EEG (which stands for electroencephalogram).

Sue took Brian to the recommended EEG lab, where Brian interrupted the script by locking himself in the men's room. He objected to what was about to be done with him. He was scared.

The EEG confirmed Dr. Marshall's suspicions, and he called to tell us.

"I'm sorry to inform you that Brian has temporal lobe epilepsy," he said. This came as quite a blow to Sue, as she had read the book *Violence and the Brain*, by Vernon Mark and Frank Ervin, in connection with her academic work. It makes the connection between violent behavior and temporal lobe epilepsy.

And yet we grasped at this hypothesis as if reaching for a life preserver. Brian did as well. He knew that during these episodes he was not in control of his own behavior, and was as troubled as we were about his condition.

Over the next several years we struggled mightily to understand what was going on with Brian and how we could help. It was not just a seizure disorder. His brain function was impacted more broadly. Though we sometimes felt our struggles were unique, other parents have gone through what we have. We were seeing the usual parenting issues, only in more extreme form. On the other hand, Brian did face some unique challenges that were quite daunting in their complexity, tenacity, and intractability.

We were determined to chart a path forward for our family and for Brian. The turning point came when we shifted our understanding from the behavioral model to the neurological model. In the behavioral model, we are in the world of good and bad. This is where we were when Brian was expelled, only Brian was so down on himself that the good/bad divide in his mind became good versus evil. In the neurological model, we are in the realm of the functional versus the dysfunctional. These two perspectives needed to be merged somehow for Brian to get on with life.

Brian's decision to live, which was quite real, came through the realization that he was more than the sum of his bad behaviors. He was not the person other people saw. He hated these external manifestations of his brain dysfunctions, and rejected them. "I am not my personality," he declared. The neurological life preserver allowed him to say, to himself and to others, "It's not really me. It's my brain." His core self was sound and whole and good. It deserved to live on.

The journey ahead had us tip-toeing through a minefield. Brian lived at the edge of explosive violence and of neurological breakdown. He was a risk to himself and to others. When we left Roscomare Road School for the last time, we began traveling an uncharted path. Indeed, no conventional path was left open to us.

Despite myriad brain dysfunctions that could even be life-threatening, Brian lived another fourteen years. After achieving the independent life that we hardly thought possible, Brian ultimately succumbed to a nocturnal seizure during his last year of college. His successful battle with so much misfortune was ultimately championed not just by us, but by him. We had no idea of the extent of his determination until after his death.

Among a mere handful of possessions Brian left us in his room at Cal Poly San Luis Obispo, the most precious was his journal. Clearly written for his own eyes, the journal chronicles his interior journey, the ongoing struggles against his brain dysfunctions. We knew that it was important to him that his life experience be shared. His hope was to educate others about his condition, and through his journal he has done just that.

As I now complete this book, I am struck by Salman Rushdie's reflections on his own journal from the days of his fatwa, when he was living under the official threat of assassination. Rushdie writes, "Sometimes I was very heartened by what I found, and sometimes I thought the person writing the journal was clearly in a very bad state of mind, very depressed or very angry or just kind of unbalanced in some way."

The same could be said about Brian's journal. Only in this case it was a child, adolescent, and young adult who had to come to terms with an unbalanced and unstable brain. Brian's journal is very raw, and ranges far afield. The normal fears and anxieties of childhood and the highs and lows of adolescence are exaggerated, until in early adulthood a more stable personality is very purposefully crafted.

It is a rare gift to gain insight into the life of a growing child who faces extreme challenges on his own because the world around him just does not understand. Brian grapples with fundamental questions, with issues of good versus evil, self versus non-self, the boundary between control and acceptance, the anticipation of death, and the constraints on our free will. Finally, Brian's journal is about the growth of the capacity for relationship, about the assertion of independence, about the setting of life goals, and about reaching clarity on our essential nature.

# 1

## THE TROUBLE WITH BRIAN

1968–1985

*My life goal as I saw at an early age was to learn and understand how nature works, and to teach that to others. By nature I mean all sciences underlying how it works. I, of course, do not expect to fully understand nature, nor do I claim to be right. I am always open to others' ideas, and there is always more to learn.*

Brian's journal [July 6, 1989]

### A DIFFICULT BIRTH

*I was born in Ithaca, New York in October 1968. I lived there for two years.*

Brian's journal [Fall 1986]

In 1968 it was still the dark ages in terms of childbirth. Sue was alone in a small, unadorned labor room in Tompkins County Hospital. I was allowed an occasional, brief visit, but otherwise Sue was alone with her labor pains. The instructions we had been given were that all would be taken care of. Just come to the hospital.... We had of course seen the films. At least I had been exposed to them. I did not sit through them all, not having mastered my own squeamishness. But these films dealt with the facts, and somehow did not convey all of the reality of childbirth.

It was October 7, near the peak of fall colors in Ithaca, New York. In past years, we would have taken long hikes on Connecticut Hill at about this time, to enjoy the explosion of color before the quagmire of ambivalent winter descended upon Cayuga Lake. We were both in graduate school at Cornell, but we were finished with all classroom work, so our schedules were somewhat under our control. Having children was really not yet on the schedule at all.

We had no idea that Sue was pregnant nine months earlier when she appeared to have a severe case of the flu, and could keep down no food, and ultimately no water either. After about four days, Sue went to the hospital, and the pregnancy was diagnosed. The doctor from the Cornell student health services told her, "You probably knew it all the time." Sue was furious. It was only the first of many such gratuitous indignities. When I first visited Sue in the hospital after the "diagnosis," and was turning to leave, she said: "You're leaving us!" This had the intended effect. It brought home to me that Sue's priorities had suddenly changed. Our self-absorbed, cerebral existence was thudding to earth, tethered by biological necessity.

What Sue was going through was no mere morning sickness. This was nausea morning, noon, and night. Tigan® became part of her regular diet, so that she could keep down her food for the duration of the pregnancy. This medication is intended to deal with nausea and vomiting. Its use during pregnancy has declined over the years as medical options proliferated, but it had been a lifesaver for us.

When Sue was finally wheeled into the delivery room, the obstetrician was busy with another delivery on the other operating table. And

when Sue was about to give birth, he yelled over to her to wait! That's like yelling at a Pacific storm. Just how does one wait, when a baby is ready be born? This is not a time when a woman feels in command of what is happening.

When it was finally Brian's turn to be conveyed into this world, he was frightfully blue. However, the obstetrician remained of good cheer. After a few minutes, Brian was pink like he was supposed to be. We were alarmed, but pacified by the soothing voice of the obstetrician. Still, Sue was concerned enough to mention Brian's "blue period" when we finally had a chance to talk.

In retrospect, we were not very original with our choice of names. "Brian" seemed refreshingly different at the time, but the same thought must have been going through the minds of an entire generation of parents, because in his age range there turned up a lot of Brians. We picked "Eugene" as the middle name. It held no intrinsic attraction for us, but we did it in resonance with the maverick presidential campaign of Eugene McCarthy. Sue's major advisor, Professor Frank Rosenblatt, played a role in that campaign. If Brian had some of McCarthy's Irish stubbornness, independence of mind, and sheer pluck, that would not be all bad. Sue was a FitzGerald, after all. We were probably too insensitive to the fact that we had burdened Brian with the initials BEO, or BO for short. Yikes.

## FATHERHOOD

*I look at my father with an angry expression, and he looks at me with an angry expression. We hardly ever communicate.*

**Brian's journal [August 11, 1990]**

Fatherhood did not come naturally to me. I was essentially an only child. My only brother is 16 years younger, and I was off to college before he was one year old. I was willing to be patient, however, until Brian grew up to be a person who could be engaged with meaningfully. That this was an individual with unique features and quirks and personality from day one, and not merely a generic baby, was something I had to learn. I did not reach this point with a good model of fatherhood.

I did not meet my own father until I was eleven years old. That was due to very unusual circumstances indeed. I was born in Berlin, Germany in 1940, during the first year of World War II. My father was encouraged to leave Germany by the American Embassy shortly after his wedding because the clouds of war were gathering, and American citizens could no longer be assured protection. After the war, repatriation to the US was problematic. My mother was still a German citizen, and as such would hardly be welcome in the US in the immediate postwar environment. It took years for arrangements to be made, and even at the last minute my mother had to stay behind as I flew by myself to meet my father in New York.

My father was not there to meet me when I arrived at Idlewild Airport. My flight had been delayed to the point where he had returned to the city, awaiting notice from the airline that was not forthcoming. I wiled away the time looking at a tele-handwriting machine when I was suddenly embraced from behind. I hardly recognized the man from his pictures. My first thought was of being kidnapped. But he knew German pretty well. Maybe he was my father, after all. It was Christmas Eve, 1951. We stayed at the YMCA downtown, and were driven down to Richmond next day in a funny-looking Studebaker that looked like it was going the wrong way.

Given that I grew up without my father, each of us undoubtedly held an idealized view of the other. Apparently I disappointed him, once the actualized reality stood before him. The problem is that by the time one is eleven years old, the mold is pretty well cast. My father's belated attempts to remake the mold only caused conflict. Child-raising is a two-way process, one in which the child effectively teaches the parents—by trial and error—how he is most successfully parented. I had not had the opportunity to "raise my father," so to speak, with the result that he proceeded on the basis of abstract principle, derived no doubt from his own harsh upbringing. The absence of my mother in the early months likely contributed to things getting off on the wrong track.

My mother's parenting style had been totally different. It was much more gentle and accommodating. Perhaps this had something to do with the fact that we had been through thick and thin together during the war years and afterwards. The bond of dependency had forged a close relationship.

My father and I had only a few years together before I left for college, and he died of pancreatic cancer soon thereafter. Those few years had been difficult, and there was no opportunity later for the relationship to evolve. In sum, then, I did not have a good model of fatherhood to go on.

## EARLY SIGNS

*At age two I had a vision of my goal in life.
That vision, however, left me.*

Brian's journal [November 23, 1989]

Brian started out auspiciously enough to meet any nervous new parents' expectations. He had come to us years ahead of schedule, but now that we had him, we also couldn't wait for him to walk and talk. Whereas his physical coordination was excellent, he was slow to talk. A dear friend who was in child development observed weightily that Brian was a "head-banger," making us nervous about what the implications of that might be. Beyond that, Brian seemed to function normally as far as we—his biased parents—could judge.

However, one time as I was checking on Brian after we'd put him to bed, he seemed to be looking at me without seeing me. This trance-like state sent chills down my spine. Sue and I talked about what I had seen. Sue's field of graduate study was neurobiology, so I was hoping for a professional opinion. Sue dismissed the significance of what I had witnessed. Odd things can happen during sleep onset. Infant sleep is not yet well-organized. Etc. We never saw anything like that again for several years, so the memory faded. Only much later, when Brian's temporal lobe epilepsy was diagnosed, did we unearth this memory as perhaps a related phenomenon.

Another factor was involved, no doubt, in Sue's dismissal of what I had seen. There is a lot of built-in resistance to confronting the question of whether something may be wrong with your child. The issue is on your mind all along, starting with counting all fingers and toes on the first day. But you are really not prepared for anything but normalcy until the issue forces itself upon you. Disabilities and dysfunctions are simply not issues that can be discussed like others, such as whether Turkey should be allowed to join the European Union.

Meanwhile, we were thrilled at Brian's progress. Practically his first word was "moon," and we marveled at his powers of abstraction when he correctly identified the sliver of new moon also as "moon." This was the time of the moon landings, July of 1969, when NASA published its first pictures of "Earthrise" over the moon's horizon taken by Neil Armstrong, Edwin "Buzz" Aldrin, and Michael Collins. On seeing the pictures, Brian declared the Earth, too, was "moon," and it was pointless to insist that this picture was in fact taken from the moon. He was only nine months old, for heaven's sake!

Brian practically lived in the Gerry carrier, which allowed us to go hiking and cross country skiing in the Ithaca area, and even to undertake a trip to the Alps in the fall, when he was eleven months old. On one eventful skiing trip, I fell forward on the skis into four feet of snow. Brian was catapulted out of the Gerry and planted head-first into the snow, with only his legs sticking out. At this point, I was looking up at my skis, which were still on top of the snow. Righting oneself from that position is not quickly done. Meanwhile, Brian had a bit of a scare about whether he would ever have a chance to breathe again. I plucked him out of the snow as quickly as I could, and he was fine.

## LOS ANGELES

*In 1970, my father got an offer for a job in Los Angeles, so my family moved there. At the age of two I was very interested in the woods behind my house, but not going more than a mile away by myself. I remember liking to climb tall trees at about the age of four.*

Brian's journal [Fall 1986]

In the fall of 1970 we moved to Los Angeles. I had just received my Ph.D. in experimental physics. There was a recession in aerospace at the time, and jobs for new physics Ph.D.s were scarce. Horror stories were circulating about newly minted physics Ph.D.s applying for high-school teaching jobs in small towns in Texas.

Sue was still working on her Ph.D. at Cornell's Langmuir Laboratory, but I feared that job openings were only going to get scarcer with the passage of time. I started working at the Northrop Research and Technology Center under Dr. Orlie Curtis, the physicist for whom I had previously worked at the Oak Ridge National Laboratory during my undergraduate years at Virginia Polytechnic Institute. When I arrived at my new job, my assigned chair was still warm from the guy who had been laid off the previous Friday.

It was easy to fall in love with Los Angeles. First of all, coming from cloudy Ithaca it was a great event to wake up to blue skies nearly every day. Initially it was, "Brian, come look at the blue sky." Not long thereafter, however, it became, "Brian, come take a look at this pretty cloud." We seemed to be the only users of the motel pool, which we assumed had been heated to 70 degrees. The exotic plants, the proximity of the desert, of the mountains, and of the ocean—all these things quickly dispelled any reservations we had about coming here from the State of New York.

We settled into a house in the Santa Monica Mountains, in Sherman Oaks. Actually, the house took some getting used to. The roof leaked. We had not specifically asked about that when we bought it, carelessly assuming that a roof is a roof is a roof. Not in Southern California. Also you could hear every raindrop hit the roof before it came into the house. There was no ceiling insulation. That was not all. Every window rattled when an airplane or helicopter passed overhead. Our house was in the flight path of Van Nuys airport, the busiest general aviation airport in the country. The louvered windows leaked heat so badly that one end of the house could be unaware that there was a quarter million BTU heater working away at the other end. We began to appreciate that the Southern California lifestyle is partly a life of the mind; i.e., a fantasy. You ignore the rain and the cold, and you can sound persuasive telling others that it doesn't rain or get cold here. Truth be told, we have winters here where we get more rain in three months than Portland gets all year. And the limp, discolored leaves of the agave tell you that it can freeze here as well.

We learned that the brush around here routinely burns, putting houses at hazard, and that the earth swells and heaves with the heavy rains, gradually leading to cracked pools, and occasionally sending them down the hillsides. We had not been in the house three months yet when the Sylmar earthquake hit. I instinctively ran to Brian's room, scooped him up, and swept him outside. If the rain-saturated hillside above our house were to give way, his room was at greatest risk.

The experience of an earthquake reminds one of how basic our assumptions are about terra firma. It goes a lot deeper than our conscious awareness. The earth rolls and jolts, the house makes an infernal racket, and cabinets vomit their contents. It was difficult for me not to take this personally. Maybe this is because the millimeter veneer of pre-frontal

neocortex does not stand a chance against the limbic system, our emotional core, which can feel assaulted.

It would be a long time before this house, this glorified tent, would truly be considered home, its tantrum forgiven. On the other hand, I began to see a certain utility in building tents in earthquake country, much like the Japanese have done for a long time. It was masonry walls and chimneys that tended to collapse in earthquakes. Our spare plasterboard walls simply yielded to all the jostling.

It took trips back East for both Sue and me to realize how much adjustment had in fact taken place in our acceptance of this transient quality of our existence. Sue had gone back to Ithaca to attend the funeral of her major advisor, Frank Rosenblatt, who died in a sailing accident in Chesapeake Bay. And I had gone back to Richmond with Brian to see his grandmother. The red brick houses of Richmond, and the Civil War statues on Monument Avenue, where we used to live, evoked a sense of permanence that clearly informs the expectations of local residents. No earthquakes here. Los Angeles, by contrast, does not live by history. It does not so much exist as a definable entity, but rather is always becoming. So few of the people we met on a daily basis were rooted here that it all seemed a mere convergence of varied agendas. The felt impermanence of our house buttressed this experience of transience in our life.

## WANDERINGS

*I often isolated myself in the woods to think. I would sit for hours at a time, alone, searching for answers. I searched for an answer to where I was headed in life.*

Brian's journal [October 30, 1989]

For Brian, the location was ideal in that it gave him the physical freedom he had previously enjoyed in Ithaca. The house was surrounded by chaparral that he could explore at will, and the pool turned him into an aquatic animal. He seemed to take advantage of this freedom rather more than we expected. One morning he was out before breakfast. We found him in his pajamas at the top of the steep hill behind our house. On another occasion, he had not returned to the yard after some hours. We searched the hillside and the neighborhood. Some hours later, a woman came to our door with Brian in tow. He was dirty and disheveled. The woman wanted to verify that Brian in fact belonged to this household. She asked a lot of questions. She was obviously reluctant to leave him with such neglectful parents. Neglectful? We had chosen the house for its unfenced yard and the freedom to roam that it promised.

On another occasion, Brian appeared at our backdoor with a neighbor from the next street at the top of the hill. On this occasion, Brian had managed to reach yet another backyard after playing in the chaparral. He wasn't talking much yet, so the concerned neighbor decided to see Brian back to his house. Brian couldn't tell him the street address,

so the fellow followed Brian back through the brush. This was an easy matter for a short two-year-old, but a bit of a chore for a tall man, who needed to crawl on his hands and knees to get through the thicket.

On yet another occasion, Brian was again absent for too long, and I set out in search of him. While I was still combing the hills, I heard a fire engine passing by in full cry. It crossed my mind that Brian might have had something to do with this, but I suppressed the thought. By the time I got back home, there was nothing left but to tell me the tale. Brian had climbed up on a local cliff, where he had never gone before. He was quite in charge of himself, and not at all afraid. A neighbor saw him on the cliff, however, and told him to stay put with great urgency. He called the fire department, and a fireman was lowered down by rope to rescue him. Brian assured us that he was never in any danger—he did not consider himself a risk-taker. He enjoyed the whole thing so much we were afraid he would try the same thing again. He spared us that.

During this time, it was comforting to know that we were not the only ones to whom things like this happened. *The Los Angeles Times* reported the story in which the police picked up a two-year-old who was window shopping on Ventura Boulevard in Woodland Hills in the middle of the night. They took him home in their police cruiser, and left the child in the car while they identified the parents, and then berated them for being so neglectful of their child. While they were still talking to the parents, a second police cruiser drove up to the house, with the same child in it. He had, in the interim, scrambled out of the first police car and made his way back to Ventura Boulevard, only to be intercepted by the second crew. We were learning fast.

## SCHOOL

*In kindergarten, I made a lot of friends. Now five years old, I walked up to three miles from home.*

*I walked to my girlfriend's house three miles away. I never thought of the possibility that she might not be home, but she was always there when I went to her house.*

Brian's journal [Fall 1986]

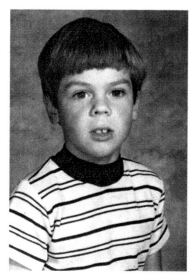

Brian attended a neighborhood pre-school. The teachers liked him well enough, but it was clear that they were often exasperated by him. We were delicately informed by the staff that when it came to doing hop, skip, and jump, "When the others are on jump, Brian is still on hop." He was on his own path, and operated by his own lights.

When it came to first grade, we were uncertain that Brian was ready. The public school he was to attend was Roscomare Road School, filled with the sharp, sophisticated children of striving upper middle class parents. The first-grade teacher encouraged us to start him, and we did. We should not have. Although Brian was bright enough, he had trouble staying with the agenda. He did not actively participate in the class.

This got much worse in the second grade. He was essentially a non-participant, and sat in the back of the class. By itself, this was not a problem as far as the school was concerned. After all, someone has to be in the bottom half of the class. But it did seem strange to us.

In the third grade he had a very kind teacher from an inner city school. When she could not say anything nice about a child, she preferred to say nothing at all. So we didn't hear about the fact that Brian's academic performance continued to go downhill.

# KAREN

*When I started elementary school, first grade went very well. In second grade, something had changed me drastically. I had no friends at the school. I no longer was making friends. My sister had died a few months before at the age of fourteen months, due to a brain tumor. I was so depressed because of her death that I was osing control of my feelings and behavior. It resulted in me fighting all the time at school. It became a big problem and I couldn't stop. I even became suicidal.*

Brian's journal [Fall, 1986]

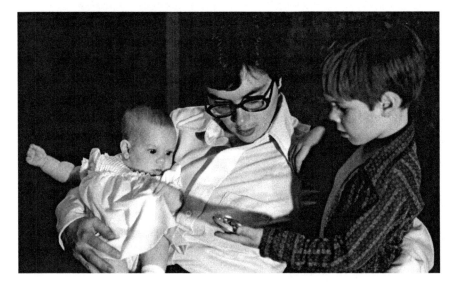

The death of his baby sister may indeed have had something to do with what Brian was going through, so it is important to recount this history. Karen was born in December of 1973. It had been another difficult pregnancy for Sue, and this time it was Bendectin® rather than Tigan that pulled her through the incessant nausea. Questions had not yet been raised about the safety of Bendectin. A certain level of risk would have been acceptable. Sue could not keep any food or drink down without it. It was that, or lose the pregnancy.

After some months, Karen developed difficulties in keeping down food. We took her to our pediatrician, Dr. Robert Marshall, who was very concerned but kept his own counsel as to what he thought was going on. He muttered something about Bell's palsy, because one side of Karen's face was showing some signs of distortion, of partial paralysis.

Despite the mounting concerns, and with Marshall's blessing, we undertook a family vacation to Montana. There Karen's difficulties in keeping down food worsened. An old retired general practitioner examined her—far removed from civilization—and encouraged us to seek further help.

"She is not thriving," he said.

That certainly put a benign face on matters that seemed more ominous.

Dr. Marshall was out of reach on his annual vacation. In Missoula, Montana, the medical staff of the hospital considered pyloric stenosis. This condition is a narrowing of the pylorus, the opening of the stomach into the small intestine. It is typically identified in infants of this age (six months), although at the time it had not been reported in girl babies. An operation was performed to relieve the muscular constraints on the pylorus, and indeed her symptoms improved. However, the problem had clearly not been entirely resolved, and now a more severe neurological problem had to be considered.

We returned with Karen to Los Angeles and took her directly to the UCLA Medical Center in Westwood. The resident came to take her history at four in the morning. He was clearly struggling to stay awake. These were the days before CAT scans and MRIs. Karen underwent a number of procedures to explore what might be going on in her brain, including a pneumoencephalogram, a very painful procedure, and finally an exploratory operation.

An inoperable brain tumor was found. Dr. Marshall, on hearing what had transpired during his absence, said sheepishly that he just hadn't expected things to move so fast. He affected not to have been surprised by the findings.

Karen was also attended by the pediatric neurologist John Menkes, of "Menkes Syndrome" fame. (That's a genetic disorder affecting regulation of copper, which is needed for various enzymes. The disorder also involves neurological deficits.) Dr. Menkes would occasionally come around with his flock of students. This was a teaching hospital, after all. He never came within six feet of Karen. For him, she remained a "case."

Karen was signed up for a series of cobalt-60 radiation treatments at UCLA. Every day, Sue would take Karen to UCLA for the treatments. Since the radiation had to be delivered very precisely to a certain area of the brain, Karen had to be kept still. This was difficult, so Karen was anesthetized. She did not react well to the chloral hydrate, which fact was duly noted in her chart. The next day, the intern reflexively went for the chloral hydrate. Karen again had a bad experience with it, and again this was duly noted in the chart. The third day, a yet different intern again went for the chloral hydrate. Sue was amazed that no one bothered to read Karen's chart. She mentioned the problem to him. Day by day, the problem recurred, and Sue had to bring the staff up to speed on each occasion. Sue was learning assertiveness as a survival strategy in impersonal hospitals. We finished Karen's radiation therapy at Cedars Sinai, where ingeniously Karen was held in a restraint normally used for babies undergoing circumcision. Karen's delicate frame was still small enough to fit.

After the radiation therapy, Karen's activity level increased markedly. She was crawling all over the floor. It was soon apparent, however, that Karen was again having difficulties. There had been only a transient suppression of tumor growth, a common outcome of radiation treatment.

Sue took Karen to UC San Francisco Medical School for chemo-therapy treatments. They had never treated a baby so young. The treatments were started at a very low level, because toxicities and tolerances had not been established for babies. Nor, for that matter, was the dosage even known. It was a complete stab in the dark.

While Sue was at UCSF, she met Ryan and his mother. Ryan's case was so unusual that it was simply referred to as Ryan's syndrome. His mother had been a nun, but she had abandoned her vows to marry an Air Force officer. She had been around hospitals so long that she had learned assertiveness as a survival tactic. Sue took lessons. Later, when Sue was deploying her skills, trying to get timely attention to Karen, the staff nurse simply brushed her off with the remark, "We're not talking about a cure, here, after all." In other words, Karen was there as an experiment, primarily in the service of science. 'Don't get your hopes up' was the message. What sets priorities here are the needs of the staff, not those of the patients. In yet another teaching and research hospital, Karen had again become a "subject" rather than a "patient."

This was a clarifying moment for Sue. Inadvertently, this brusque comment made clear that Karen's status was seen as hopeless. In fact, the fast-growing tumor did overtake events. Karen's daily care was taking more and more of Sue's resources. It became a full-time, day and night operation. Previously Karen had been such a beautiful baby that she was at risk of becoming community property in the grocery store. Now her facial distortion was causing people to avert their gaze. Karen no longer existed in public at all.

While our conscious brains were still holding on to hope, we were in fact accommodating emotionally to what was becoming inevitable. When Karen showed difficulty in breathing, Marshall suspected she was suffering from cranial pressure, so Sue returned with her to Cedars Sinai Hospital. The journey was by ambulance, siren blaring. Traffic gave way whenever it could. Dogs sat down and howled in sympathy with the siren's wail.

The next morning, Karen was examined by staff doctors. One procedure was to stick her with a pin over various parts of her body, to see where she still had sensory awareness.

"She isn't crying," said the neurologist.

"She no longer has a voice," I answered.

That is why they keep parents outside. I asked the doctor what he thought could still be accomplished. He answered that really nothing could be done anymore, that they just wanted to know what was going on. Confronted with death, even doctors may be propelled into a frantic but futile activism.

The doctor had given me the rationale for an autopsy, not anything of any remedial or supportive value. With new clarity, we came finally to the decision to cease all treatment, and to focus instead on making Karen comfortable. I had to convey this to the doctors, because Sue could not bring herself to utter those words. An unwritten hospital policy came into effect: "Do not treat."

Two hours later, Karen died in Sue's arms. She never had a chance to know what life was all about.

The doctors approached us about doing an autopsy. Almost reflexively, I said no. Karen was back with us now. The medical agenda was not in charge any more. I surprised myself by my reaction to this perfectly reasonable request—particularly since both of us were scientists. But it was as if my whole being was finally in revolt against all that had been done to Karen, that infinitely good-natured, trusting, wide-eyed little girl. We had been dealt with professionally every step of the way—with the isolated exceptions of the oblivious hospital staff at UCLA and the arrogant nurse at UCSF—but none of this medical adventure should ever have been undertaken. Here we had a rapidly growing pediatric tumor, for which there simply was no remedy in 1975. Our signatures are on all the informed consent documents, but let's face it: it had been a manufactured consent.

There had been a conspiracy of silence regarding the ultimate pointlessness of all of these undertakings. We had been led down the garden path by all that erudition.

## BRIAN AND KAREN

> *What I have said thus far explains my beliefs and goals in my early years up to age seven. But at that time my younger sister died. I could not understand why so many children teased me. My enlightened childhood was over.*
>
> Brian's journal [July 6, 1989]

Brian had of course felt left out during this outsize preoccupation with Karen. He even said at one point, "I wish I could be in the hospital so that you would take care of me." Now his abandonment was perhaps even worse, because we were preoccupied with our own grief. Probably he had sometimes wished Karen out of his life, in classic sibling pattern, and now he had his wish! Undoubtedly he was blaming himself for her death at some level. In any case, we had no awareness of what internal emotional crisis he was going through as a result of Karen's sudden disappearance.

Regrettably in retrospect, we arranged for no ceremony. Such an event might have helped Brian to accommodate Karen's sudden disappearance, and it might have helped us to recognize his state of bewilderment and sense of loss.

It was February, 1975. Brian was in first grade. We remember doing all of the usual things in the months following Karen's death. We took Brian to see the famous mime Marcel Marceau at the Shubert Theatre. During the following summer, we went to the Hollywood Bowl, to Catalina Island, to the LaBrea tar pits, to Sea World in San Diego, and to the Laserium at the Griffith Park Observatory. We also visited Tuolumne Meadows in Yosemite. In the fall, we went to Montana on vacation.

At the Hollywood Bowl we attended an Elton John concert. We were up in the cheap seats, and Brian still managed to fall asleep despite the volume of sound. As he was splayed out in my arms in slumber, he wet his pants...! We were mortified, standing by utterly helpless as the stream dribbled down progressively (and in such volume!) from one ledge to the next. We were hundreds of yards away from the nearest men's room. With the benefit of hindsight, one might ask whether this was perhaps another early sign of the neurological problems to come. After all, we were way past the time when bed-wetting had been an issue.

The trip to Tuolumne Meadows in particular was memorable. Brian and I climbed the front face of Lembert Dome, that bald granite boulder which was smoothed by glacial action. Where you face it from the parking lot, the rise is so steep that ropes are required. But slightly south of that area, the mountainside is less steep, and one can simply climb at the limit of adhesion of one's boots. Brian was awfully reluctant at first. I reassured him: the worst that could happen was that one would slide down on one's bottom to where the slope was less steep. Brian came along cautiously. We reached a terraced portion of the mountain, where the rocks had a rough washboard structure. We climbed from terrace to terrace. By the time we reached our goal, Brian had lost all his fear. He came back down triumphant, a confirmed mountain climber.

There is no recollection of anything that year being seriously amiss with Brian. Sue was undergoing yet a third difficult pregnancy, quickly to fill the void that had been left. Kurt was born to us that November.

## BAD BEHAVIOR

> *Life was beautiful when I was young, until I underwent an evil change in personality and beliefs.*

Brian's journal [September 23, 1989]

It is difficult to reconstruct the sequence of events from memory, but we began to see Brian's behavior deteriorating in a number of ways. He would get into occasional fights, and on one day Brian told us that the kids at the bus stop had stuffed him into a trashcan. Since other kids were not getting stuffed into trashcans, Brian probably was at least partly responsible. Brian was becoming a rather sullen and unhappy child. As reports of his bad behavior continued to come home, we became increasingly concerned. "Just what do we have to do, Brian? This behavior has to stop."

At this point, Brian said disarmingly: "I guess I'm just an evil person. I'm just going to go to prison when I grow up."

We were blown away. This out of the mouth of an eight-year-old. One wanted to back up and start the conversation all over again. "No, Brian, you are not an 'evil' person. It's just that some of your behavior is simply intolerable. You will simply have to learn to control your behavior."

"I don't understand, Mom. If prison isn't for people like me, who is it for?"

We had only standard behavioral models to guide us, and these placed the burden squarely on Brian—and on ourselves. It was all up to us to sort out and manage. But Brian was ahead of us in one respect. He already knew that that was out of the question. He simply wasn't in control of his own behavior. And yet the behaviors looked ever so willful to any outside observer: hurling obscenities at people; picking fights at the slightest provocation; scratching someone's face. How can that not be intentional behavior?

We were perhaps a bit slow to pick up on all the changes because Brian could be very different at home. There he would simply disappear into the chaparral behind our house and absent himself from those disagreeable human contacts that were triggers for him. One could almost say that we were seeing two aspects of the fight-flight response. It was flight at home, where that option was available to him, and fight at school, where it wasn't. Given the choice, he would absent himself from problematic situations. Therein lay a hopeful clue.

*If I was going to stay alive, I had to do my best to contain this bad side to my personality. I despised this evil spirit in me so highly, that if I was going to live at all it was not going to be nice. I tried to eradicate humor from myself so that anger or other uncontrollable feelings would not exist either. If I could eliminate emotions, my problem would be eliminated. I isolated myself from*

*people so as to prevent any problems from aris-*
*ing. I decided to devote my life to understanding*
*myself, this problem, and hopefully solving it.*

*Two years after the start of this change in*
*personality, I concluded that the problem was*
*not solvable, and that I would never have any*
*friends. I was now nine years old. It was also at*
*this time that I decided it would be necessary*
*to devote my whole life to this problem. I had*
*lost all the friends I had a few years a back, or*
*so I thought. Since I believed I had no friends, I*
*naturally didn't.*

Brian's journal [September 23, 1989]

Brian was way ahead of us. He was aware that he was not in control of his behavior. It was not a matter of willpower. He was probably right also that people with similar problems do fill the prisons. He was not telling us this as a way of getting us to get off his case. This was an honest struggle to understand himself and his interactions with a world that so strongly disapproved of him. Brian frequently considered suicide. After we had had another argument about his behavior, he told us in resignation, "I'm just going to kill myself." This was not a fresh thought. He had clearly run this through his mind many times before. Again, he was not saying this to get us to back off. Instead, it was saying, "You're right. I'm so awful that I can't claim to have any right to be alive." On another occasion, he pronounced to us that he was a "warlock." Brian was relatively non-verbal. And this was not a word in common usage. Where did he possibly latch onto such a notion? The concept of warlock was to him a framework in which some of his behavior could make sense.

## EXPLOSIVE ANGER

*People thought I was a naughty child trying to deceive them. Only I could realize that something more subtle had caused me to do things without intending to do them. My angry emotions on the surface of my "self" were all people saw, but deeper within the "self" I was still loving people and life. I lost all my friends, and the only answer was for me to find the "way" through my own search.*

Brian's journal [October 30, 1989]

Outside of school there were other crises. We joined some Sierra Club outings because Brian seemed to do best in the outdoor environment. He also functioned better with adults than with his peers. Sierra Club members also seem more tolerant of the diversity in the human species. The Natural Science Section of the Angeles Chapter was a particularly congenial refuge. Sue had become an outings leader there. Brian was fascinated by natural phenomena, and here was a congregation of folk who shared these interests. The Natural Science Section offered Field Ecology Workshops that entire families could attend. There was even a program especially tailored for children. After Brian attended the one of those, however, they were discontinued.... I was afraid to ask why...

On another occasion, we attended a Sierra Club picnic in Malibu Creek State Park. Seemingly out of the blue, Brian was suddenly beating up a little girl in her Sunday whites. I rushed over to restrain him, and out of the corner of my eye saw the girl's father approaching with vengeance in his eyes. I demonstratively gave Brian a spanking to assuage the man's wrath, and to forestall his personal intervention. The spanking was largely pre-emptive. After the way I had been raised, with severe physical punishment well-remembered, I was determined not to propagate that to our children. But if spanking is ever justified, surely it is in response to violence being done to another child. In the moment, of course, the spanking also served to vent my own frustration, and to compensate for my sense of helplessness. I had in fact incorporated the template for my reflexive response from my own upbringing. We left, utterly shaken. Brian had no explanation to offer for what had happened.

Shortly thereafter, Sue took Brian to the shoe store. A child was sitting next to him, also waiting for service with his mom. Suddenly, Brian started to punch the child mercilessly. Sue quickly restrained him. When asked for an explanation, Brian said that he didn't like the way the other child was looking at him.

Brian was also playing T-ball at the local Sherman Oaks Park. Brian was appreciated for his hitting, but other aspects of the game were not his strength. Two incidents stand out. On one occasion the team gathered for a team photo. I had taken my eyes off the group for only a moment, but when I looked back the boy standing next to Brian had tears rolling down his face. He tried not to show his pain. He had probably taken a rabbit punch from Brian the instant I had taken my eyes off the group. Brian stood there looking somewhat angry, but clearly anxious not to give himself away.

On another occasion, Sue and I were both present to watch the game. As it came time to leave, we got into one of the increasingly frequent arguments with Brian. He did not want to leave just yet. His oppositional behavior evolved into an episode in which Brian fell down on the ground and made strange noises. We were mortified. The rest of the crowd mercifully continued to act as if nothing out of the ordinary were happening. We got Brian off the ground and hustled him off to the car. This did not seem to be the kind of behavior that Brian would indulge in voluntarily. And yet the whole thing flowed seamlessly from beginning to end. Just what was going on? If Brian had been younger, this behavior would have been dismissed as an ordinary tantrum. But throwing himself on the ground at his age certainly seemed odd.

We got a call from the school asking for a conference. We had heard nothing from the school for some time, so we did not know what to expect. We were met with a whole committee of school officials, all solemnly arrayed facing the two of us. One after another they dumped their complaints on us about Brian's behavior. There were the fights during recess, first of all, and Brian was hurling obscenities in class, and insulting the teachers. The tenor of this barrage was that clearly our parenting skills were suspect. We were assumed to be the cause of it all. Just what did we have to say for ourselves? It was as if we were being subjected to a serial firing squad.

The school suggested a professional evaluation, and on that basis were willing to allow Brian stay in school provisionally. For their part, they would assign a resource person to him who would give him the love, affection, and attention that he clearly needed, and which was apparently lacking at home. This came straight out of the Bruno Bettel-heim school of parenting, which posited that cold and unloving parents were causally responsible for behaviorally disordered children.

## DIAGNOSIS

*It was epilepsy. I almost got expelled from the school in third grade. I was told that if it was a disease that was causing this behavior, and it could be fixed by medicine, or some other way, then I could stay, otherwise I would be expelled. I had tried very hard for two years to stop this behavior, but it never worked.*

Brian's journal [Fall, 1989]

We related all this to the pediatrician, Dr. Marshall, who suspected that epilepsy might be responsible for the behavior. Temporal lobe epilepsy often involves adverse behaviors as well as seizure activity. (In retrospect, we realize just how rare this insight was among MDs at the time. Even decades later this question was still being debated among neurologists.) We told Dr. Marshall about the time we came in to see his substitute doctor a year earlier to tell him about the auras that Brian was seeing, the intense, false colors which surrounded objects in his field of vision. The substitute doctor had not given us any indication that this was a matter of concern warranting further investigation. Also, he had either not recorded this report in the chart, or Dr. Marshall had not seen it on his return. Marshall now saw this as clear confirming evidence of seizure activity. We had lost a year.

There were other things. I told Dr. Marshall that sometimes Brian walked around the house in his sleep. He could not be awakened during these episodes. One time he even peed in the bathtub during such an episode. At other times, he had what seemed like night terrors. He would jerk violently in his bed, even sit up and bark strangely. He could not be awakened during these times. When I heard Brian begin his thrashing behavior, I would simply sit with him so that he could not hurt himself by hitting the edge of the bed or the wall. Sometimes this happened several times during the night.

If any of these strange happenings had had a dramatic onset, we probably would have become alarmed and done something sooner. The nighttime behaviors, however, had been going on for years, starting out somewhat innocuously and only gradually getting worse. We had heard of sleepwalking, of course. Perhaps this was just one of the things that parents have to put up with, like bedwetting. We had heard of night terrors, too. It just seemed to be one other thing we had to manage as parents.

Now that we surveyed the whole picture at one sitting, it all began to make some sense. What we thought were night terrors were more likely night-time seizures, and the day-time behavior was also seizure-like in character (later we learned that this is called sub-clinical seizure activity). Brian was not fully in control, but also not fully unconscious—just what he was telling us.

## DILANTIN

*When I was told that this was epilepsy, and I was supposed to take medicine (Dilantin), I was angry. First of all, I did not believe that being unable to control my behavior was due to disease; and second, how is medicine going to change my ability to control my behavior? I still put just as much effort into controlling myself as before, as if the medicine wouldn't do anything. There was a drastic change in my behavior with the medication, and I was in control of myself again.*

Brian's journal [Fall, 1989]

Dr. Marshall prescribed an anti-convulsant medication for Brian: Dilantin. The night-time seizure activity stopped almost immediately. We allowed ourselves to breathe a sigh of relief. Perhaps we were onto something. The day-time behaviors, however, continued as before. Dr. Marshall proceeded to try some other medications. One after another was found to be ineffective in dealing with this problem. Brian tried Phenobarbital. It made everything worse. He became more hyperactive. He took off walking across town, and one morning was found on our roof at sun-up, happily lighting matches while sitting there in his pajamas. Panicked, we went back to Dr. Marshall, who did not seem surprised at our report. Said Sue, "Either we change the medication, or we need a ball-and-chain."

*At age nine, when I started taking Dilantin, I experienced immediate degradation in academic performance at school. Following this, I put less effort towards using those areas of my brain which became fogged because of the medication. My ability in English work was poor, and I started to care no more. But when Dilantin was eliminated from my medication, I experienced a return of skills long lost. Still on Tegretol, I now feel the fogging effects of Tegretol. But my ability to write is showing up more and more. I expect to be doing even better once I get off Tegretol.*

*Much of the revitalizing of my writing skills occurred while I felt the urge to become right-handed. By writing with my right hand, I have brought back many mental processes to aid in writing.*

Brian's journal [November 3, 1989]

## TEGRETOL

Dr. Marshall really wanted Brian on Tegretol. However, that was an experimental medication at the time, and he was required to evaluate all the approved alternatives first, before prescribing Tegretol. So we were going down the list, one by one. In the meantime, the staff counselor at the school was doing her best to be nice to Brian. It seemed to make no difference to his behavior. When he finally hurled an obscenity at her as well, she took that as the final straw and rejected him. She was through with her manipulative display of ersatz affection. It was not surprising. It's hard to keep an act like that going. The next time we met, we got only icy stares from her. In some way, she felt us responsible for sabotaging her efforts. If Brian was unable to respond to her kind ministrations, then his emotional resources had clearly atrophied—and we were probably at fault. Monsters!

Brian was beginning to respond to the Tegretol, as his medication dose was gradually increased. He had no more violent episodes at that time, and he was just a bit easier to live with. Nevertheless, we had clearly burned our bridges with Roscomare Road School, and it was time to look for something else. A conference was set up with Los Angeles School District personnel to determine Brian's educational needs, and to select a more appropriate setting. After results of some testing became available, we drove downtown for the conference.

Brian's behavior was again an issue, but on this occasion I had in tow Brian's new brother, Kurt. Kurt charmed them all, although he gave us a challenge managing his restlessness during the conference. After witnessing how we handled Kurt during the meeting, it was simply not possible for them to indict our parenting for whatever was going on with Brian. In the end, it did not matter. The School District had only an aphasia program available, for children with speech and language learning difficulties, and that was clearly not appropriate for Brian. We had to look to the private schools.

## VISIT TO THE NEUROLOGIST

Even though Brian was now benefiting from the Tegretol, we thought it a good idea to visit a neurologist. We were already acquainted with Dr. John Menkes, and we made an appointment. Dr. Marshall was ambivalent. Perhaps he already had a good idea of what was in store for us.

Another clinical EEG was taken, and Dr. Menkes reviewed the charts. Then we met to discuss the case. We told Dr. Menkes of the night-time seizure and the sleepwalking, of the violent episodes and of the benefit we saw from the Dilantin and the Tegretol. We were unprepared for his response.

"How do you know that these are seizures?" he challenged us in a skeptical tone.

I was at a loss on how to answer him. The word seizure had only been an operative word in our vocabulary for a matter of weeks. It hadn't been my idea. It was the working hypothesis of our pediatrician, and of the neurologist who had taken Brian's first EEG. I could just deflect the question by deferring to Dr. Marshall. But that would have been a cop-out. In fact, I had become persuaded that Dr. Marshall was right, and I had assumed ownership of this hypothesis as well. So I would do my best to defend it. We went back and forth. I presented our observations, and he would dismiss them. What about the night terrors? What about the auras? Everything fit together. The atmosphere became progressively more acrimonious.

Let's not get hung up on semantics, I argued. If you want to call this something other than seizures, so be it. But what about the underlying phenomenology? Call them night terrors, seizures, auras, whatever you want. Are we not dealing here with behavior that is episodic, grossly out of character, and manifestly responsive to anti-convulsant medication? Isn't that what counts? Why do you, Dr. Menkes, feel threatened when parents make some effort to be knowledgeable about your subject? So what if we use words that for you have a precise meaning, but in our usage may not? Can't you look past that for what we are trying our level best to describe?

"I believe Brian is merely a rambunctious kid," said Menkes.

"Perhaps you should try taking him home," I thought to myself.

Menkes was among those who thought that Brian was simply react-ing to the death of Karen. He was convinced that the Tegretol level was clearly too low to be therapeutically effective. We must be dealing with a placebo effect. However, to settle the issue, he was prepared to take a blood level of Tegretol and confirm his judgment that it was below the therapeutic range. That done, he showed us the door. We were quite shaken by the verbal hazing we had received. When a high-powered neurologist wants to intimidate, he can overpower vulnerable parents at will. He wrote Dr. Marshall a letter, handwritten in perfect form remi-niscent of Sigmund Freud himself, and related his findings. A week or so later, a second letter arrived in which Dr. Menkes acknowledged the possibility that Dr. Marshall might be correct. The Tegretol level had been found to be in the therapeutic range.

We learned another lesson. Neurologists were not going to be very useful to us in dealing with this problem. Here we were dealing with the very best, and he was so unwilling to listen that we had to struggle to get a hearing for any of our observations. Menkes was off in his con-ceptual world, making rash judgments on the basis of standard wisdom within his field. He evidenced not the slightest personal engagement with his patient. In a matter of minutes, he "understood" this case and his mind slammed shut. Only data about blood levels could reopen the issue. Behavioral phenomenology was close to being irrelevant. That was all anecdotal. How could he take that seriously? The relationship of the brain and behavior was still speculative.

This experience turned out to be so impactful for us, and so trau-matic for Brian, that it colored everything that followed. Brian never again saw the inside of a neurologist's office for the purpose of seeking help for his condition.

With the door to professional help closing in our face, the primary responsibility for managing Brian's condition fell back on Sue. At least we now had the advantage of a new template, that of neurologically-mediated dysfunction. Sue ongoingly had to decide what aspects of Brian's behavior were modifiable, and what simply had to be lived with.

## OAK HILL SCHOOL

*The principal of the new school I was going to even went out of her way to tell me how good I was. But in addition to that change, there were many others. My coordination, and quick reflexes disappeared. My grades in school got worse. I had to give up T-ball and take up some other sport such as swimming.*

*I still loved this medicine for the first few years I took it, because to me, more important than good grades, and good coordination, was the ability to make friends. The medicine also destroyed memory, self-confidence, and self-esteem. Since the age of nine, I have had to live with this medicine. I really hate the medicine. I often feel that everything is hopeless. I often feel frustrated. However, whenever I don't feel frustrated with my work, I enjoy it. I love to learn, and I am very interested in the world around me.*

Brian's journal [Fall, 1989]

Sue identified Oak Hill School as a possibility for Brian. The school accepted children with learning and behavior problems. Brian's behavior was tolerable enough with the medication that that was no longer of primary concern at school. The classes were small, and the school's leadership, Herbert and Claire Lobell, were well-regarded educators with whom Sue and I felt comfortable.

One day, we heard from the school that Brian had fallen off the climbing structure and been knocked unconscious. We took him to Dr. Marshall. Brian had suffered a concussion. He was disoriented, and only slowly recovered. Marshall was concerned.

"Let me know if there are any lasting effects, such as changes in personality," he told us. "What do we do then?" we asked.

"Oh, there's really nothing that can be done. I just want to be kept informed."

Did Brian have a seizure, and did he fall as a result of that? Or had his coordination deteriorated so badly with the medication, we wondered. We were used to seeing him climb with cat-like assurance. He had been a tree-climber for years. Clearly, his physical skills had suffered with the Tegretol. At T-ball, his former skills as a power hitter were deserting him. His reaction time was slowed. His eyes had a glazed-over look of someone who wasn't all there.

## WALDORF SCHOOL

*During most of my childhood I have felt like a slave. I had to sit in front of my books every night to please my parents. I could not argue for what I wanted because my perpetual anger was already too much, without additional arguments. I lived with whatever I had or was given. If I protested too much my parents might put me in an institution for the mentally ill. All the misery, anger and fear lowered my spirits and I was often convinced I was a failure. I wondered how long I would be alive, and whether I ever would have friends.*

Brian's journal [September 12, 1989]

After Brian's second year at Oak Hill School, the management wanted to shift its focus away from learning disabled children. We wondered whether it would remain a suitable environment for Brian. He did not need to be confronted with academic failure. We came at this time to investigate a Waldorf School in Northridge, Highland Hall, for our younger son Kurt, who was ready for Kindergarten. His teachers at the Presbyterian pre-school had strongly urged us to put him on Ritalin because of his hyperactivity. We were not ready to medicate a four-year-old. At Highland Hall, they were prepared to accept him, and they were philosophically opposed to the use of such medication.

I had had my own experience with a Waldorf School shortly after World War II in Germany, having attended a residential Waldorf School in Hamborn (near Paderborn in Westfalia) prior to coming to the United States in 1951. I recalled it as by far my favorite educational experience, and was sorry to have had to leave. It was a very humane educational approach, one that was sensitive to the particular child's needs, and generously accepting of their individual differences. We were lucky to find Highland Hall open to considering taking Brian as well as Kurt. Brian went there for a spell, and they accepted him into the sixth grade. His teacher had a number of challenging children in his class. It had been his choice. Many other teachers there would not have taken on such children.

Highland Hall did for Brian exactly what was needed. It nurtured his soul. It gave him a hundred ways in which to succeed, and it did not confront him with failure. Despite his sometimes disagreeable ways, he was appreciated and valued. It kept him together until his intellect and his self-understanding could mature. Although he was probably somewhere in the middle third of the class academically, he clearly had some outstanding abilities. He just didn't have it together. That's the learning disabled child!

Brian himself was out of his mind with happiness on coming to the new school. He loved the emphasis on arts and music. The school allowed him to climb the tall eucalyptus trees - with our permission. He struggled with reading and writing, but they knew he wasn't stupid, and were willing for certain skills to come along more slowly. The school teachers seemed to be operating on a kind of Hippocratic Oath for education: "Above all, do no harm." Brian never ceased to love school, despite the sometime lack of academic success.

## BRIAN AND KURT

At home we were still facing a number of challenges. Brian was often

depressed, self-destructive, and suicidal. He could still go into rages in which he sometimes put his foot through the hollow-core doors. He would bite his own hand in self-punishment. The wrong tone of voice would set him off. He would routinely go off into the chaparral behind our house to be alone. It was difficult for him to relate to people. He seemed to be incapable of interpreting facial expressions, and therefore was in some trouble dealing with humor, with irony, and with teasing. In consequence, of course, he was relentlessly teased. The parenting challenge of containing and shaping this behavior was substantial. It called for continuous vigilance, and forbearance in great measure for Sue.

Kurt was quickly ahead of Brian in terms of understanding social situations. In fact, he often played the role of peacemaker, even at an age when he was still sitting on our laps. On the other hand, he was also hyperactive and impulsive, and could not resist stoking the volcano from time to time. It was an incendiary combination. Kurt knew how to get Brian into a snarling frenzy while appearing innocent; Brian would come down on Kurt; and we would come down on Brian. It was all very predictable. It was all very repeatable. Life was unfair.

Brian had to have a very regular, routinized existence. There was enough chaos in his life that whatever could be made orderly needed to be made orderly. He could erupt at unanticipated changes in his routine. Sue, the usual chauffeur, might for example have a visitor who would be occupying "his" seat in the car when he was being picked up from school. "What is she doing in the car?" he would say derisively, right in the presence of the visitor. It was embarrassing. We did not take the children much of anywhere, certainly not to a restaurant or to other people's homes. They were simply not fit company.

## SOFT NEUROLOGICAL SIGNS

Brian also continued to experience what are called "soft neurological signs." Sometimes his right side would feel warmer than his left. When he was feeling odd, he could not tolerate a person on his right. The person would have to be on his left. He felt that the medication simply clamped down on his occasional violent impulses. The angry thoughts still raged in his brain.

Brian continued to lag behind in his language skills, so we took him to the Speech and Language Center in Van Nuys. He also benefited from the orderliness and the ritual associated with judo, which he learned at Junior Gym from a teacher of great patience, commanding and resonant voice, and imposing bulk. Judo honed Brian's observational skills and enhanced his self-awareness. His lack of quickness (thanks to the Tegretol) he made up for with his brute strength and sheer willpower. This determination and intensity was to stand him in good stead in various trials to come.

## YOSEMITE

I accompanied Brian's seventh-grade class on their annual camping trip. The traditional site for the seventh grade trip was Yosemite. It was a chance for me to experience how Brian related to his classmates. He was clearly well accepted, but he remained the object of teasing by the other children in the class who also had problems. How intolerant we are of seeing our own weaknesses exhibited in others!

The trip was also a demonstration of the benign influence of the natural environment. Somehow the natural cathedral of Yosemite was like an anechoic chamber for conflict. It simply absorbed it, diffused it. Life assumed a more natural pace. There was elbow room for all. More could have been learned about this remarkable place. The seventh graders were caught up in a kind of frenzy occasioned by their own insecurities, and had limited attention span for geological history, glaciation, flora and fauna, etc. But the essential learning, of how to relate to one another and to the physical world, was taking place.

## MATH, SCIENCE, AND THE ARTS

The eighth grade brought participation in the class play. In a small private school, everyone must take part. Amazingly, Brian carried it off credibly. He played the role of a shady character, which to a certain extent came naturally out of his experience. In its essential aspects, however, the role remained foreign to him. Brian knew nothing of guile.

The ninth grade brought a more academic challenge. This suited Brian very well. He was drawn to the world of mathematics and the physical sciences. Here he was dealing with established laws that simply needed to be understood. There was ultimately no controversy and no ambiguity about the physical laws that he was encountering. Brian was dissatisfied with the level of physics teaching, so he simply read a college level physics text instead. This allowed him to carry on discussions with his teachers in which he was very much on a par with them. He was finding himself.

He also developed in his artistic skills, which was the school's strength, and he participated in school orchestra with his clarinet. The literary side, however, was difficult for him. The task of comparing the writing styles of three authors, for example, was beyond him. Why was it not enough simply to have read and understood the material?

His difficulties in relating to people were only compounded by the problems of teenagerdom. Socially he was simply not of the same age as his classmates. Fortunately, they accepted this, and treated him like a class mascot. He could be counted on for a certain amount of comic relief, provided in all innocence, and for the occasional oddities. He could also awe and startle them with his deep reflectiveness, his mental tenacity, and his philosophical curiosity. It was said that "Brian is good at the hard things, not so good at the easy things."

## BOND WITH THE NATURAL WORLD

Brian was gaining emotional support and intellectual sustenance from his bond with the natural world. It was a multi-faceted encounter. The relationship had a certain spiritual quality, a profound feeling dimension. He was at home there. He just simply belonged there. Nature was a cornucopia that led an inquiring mind from one puzzle to another. To a tough guy who did not mind sleeping on the ground without benefit of an air mattress, and who could eat grubs to sustain himself

without blanching at the thought, the natural world extended a generous welcome. He had become a mountain climber, and he still enjoyed
climbing trees. One approaching winter storm found Brian high up in
the sycamore in our yard, swaying back and forth in the wind, reminis
cent of that same experience recorded by John Muir in the Sierras. That
perch became a favorite place for him to go, so Brian and I constructed
a crow's nest up high in the tree where he could hang out.

Over a period of time during those years, Brian found a legitimate
outlet for his equivocal relationship to violence. He became fascinated
with knives, with camouflage, with Green Beret bravado. He possessed
a fearsomely large Bowie knife, with built-in grappling hooks, among
other such treasures. In his camouflage uniform he would truck off into
the Santa Monica and Santa Susana mountains. He encountered other
children there engaging in war games, and even met a real Vietnam veteran, one who was also isolating himself in the mountains, presumably
due to Post-Traumatic Stress Disorder. They got along famously.

There was also a time at which Brian's tree-climbing skills were very
useful. We were vacationing in Montana, and had in mind climbing

Lindy Peak in the Mission Mountains. The reclusive Charles Lindbergh had escaped to this remote place after his famous flight and the locals promptly named the mountain after him. This was grizzly country. We were aware that grizzlies were very unpredictable, but had a reputation for attacking women during their period. The Plains Indians, for example, did not allow their squaws out of the village during those times, and an attack on a number of women in Glacier Park was fresh in our memory. Our schedule was somewhat inflexible, so we decided to take our chances with Sue coming along, relying on the very low probability of actually encountering a grizzly. In the high alpine forest, however, there he suddenly was, looking at us! Arrayed in his golden brown fur, he was magnificent. And he was holding all the cards. We looked for the nearest tree to climb. The alpine conifers here had their branches growing downward, from the weight of snow and also to minimize exposure to the weather. One could not get purchase on them with one's boots. We found a broken tree onto which Sue and I could climb, and Brian had picked out a more challenging climb for himself. As we started up the tree Brian started yelling that—in his haste—he could not get his pack off quickly. Before I had even climbed back down Sue just instantly dropped down to run over and help him. Then Brian scooted up the nearest tree swiftly and without difficulty. Only after we were safely out of reach did we dare look again in the bear's direction. After all, looking at him could be taken as an aggressive gesture. He was gone.

Unfortunately, he was headed in the same direction we were. Everywhere we went we saw fresh bear signs. We continued to watch for him nervously. To put even more distance between us, we stopped for lunch on a huge boulder that gave us good visibility to all sides. A strong smell wafted in our direction, which we again took as a sign of bear. At least we were downwind from him. Moments later, two bears came crashing through the brush. They were black bears. They never saw us sitting on the rock, but passed right below us. We went on to above timberline, where we pitched tent on a patch of moss that was just the size of the tent. Brian had decided not to bring a tent, so he slept in the open on another patch of moss nearby. He would not have had it any other way. He was becoming a mountain man...a young Jeremiah Johnson...full of bravado. A tent would just have been a frivolous luxury.

Snow was our source of water. There was no tree on which to string up our food, so we sprinkled flakes of paradichlorobenzene (mothballs) around the food and sleeping areas to discourage the bears. That night, the tent was buffeted mightily by the wind. Sue remembers that I was staring at the roof of the tent, and recalls my saying, "I can think of nothing but bears!" After all, we were only a few miles from the highest concentration of grizzlies in the 49 states—in the shadow of McDonald Peak, where they go to feed on ladybird beetles.

On another occasion, we were at an IEEE (Institute of Electrical and Electronic Engineers) conference at UC Santa Cruz, which is built among the redwoods. Brian was in heaven—so many trees. At the wine and cheese party one afternoon, eyes were suddenly drawn to a boy high up in a redwood nearby. It was our son. We acted like we did not know him, and went on with our conversations. We knew full well that he was not at risk in the tall trees. Later, on the way home, we did discuss the risk involved in tree-climbing, as well as the discomfort he had caused among the people watching. Brian said with finality: "I would not take chances. I am not a daredevil. I feel perfectly secure in what I am doing." He was right, of course. He was as cautious and deliberate in his tree-climbing as in everything else. Our own discomfort about the scene that he was making, on the other hand, he could not relate to.

## HONESTY

Several vignettes from these years at Highland Hall help to characterize Brian. He once told a lie at school, and got in trouble for it. I had a long discussion with him about honesty, saying that it was worth a lot to establish a reputation for honesty, but that such a reputation could be easily undone with a lie. He took this absolutely seriously, and put it right into his "autoexec" file as an automatically executable command. He had been convinced; from that moment on, he would be scrupulously honest, and that was all there was to it. Of course, honesty did not mean that everything had to be said, necessarily. There was such a thing as diplomacy, and tact. But that was calling for too much subtlety. Brian counted on us for such honesty as well. As a result, Brian believed in Santa Claus well into High School. He simply knew us to be utterly truthful in what we told him. Once we realized this, Sue hastened to update him. The next Christmas, Brian's stocking did not go up on the mantel. He wasn't going to be held for a fool yet another time. Kurt, however, knew his stocking would be filled in the morning if only he hung it up on the mantel. As far as he was concerned, Brian had just turned from one kind of fool into another.

## BEYOND HIGH SCHOOL

By eleventh grade, Sue and I had to think beyond High School. Brian would presumably no longer be willing to live at home. Yet he was not ready for an independent life in the outside world. If he failed to take his medication, or if he was set off by some untoward event, he could conceivably go into some sort of self-destructive spiral from which he could not recover on his own resources. We began to look for institutions that would accept learning disabled college-age youth with behavior problems.

*I ran into an obstacle in my life path, and it interfered with my commitments. This brought*

*about the question of how to revise my goals
to meet the vision's expectations. Basically, I
had to eliminate whatever had possessed me
(epilepsy). I was certain that it was possible.*

Brian's journal [November 23, 1989]

## INTRODUCTION TO NEUROFEEDBACK

It was March of 1985. Sue Rosen, a friend of ours from our days at Cornell, and now living in San Francisco, had just attended the annual meeting of the ACLD (Association for Children with Learning Disabilities, which is now the LDA, or Learning Disability Association). She was also managing a severely disabled child, which drew her to the conference. With Brian in mind, she was interested in a talk by Margaret Ayers on EEG biofeedback for epilepsy. As she stood in line to pick up a tape of the talk, she found Ayers standing in front her for the same purpose. A brief conversation ensued, and then Sue Rosen hastened to call us to deliver the news. Sue was intrigued.

The technique of EEG biofeedback held out the promise that one could train the brain to function more optimally through information available in the EEG. The EEG is a measure of the electrical brainwave activity that can be picked up at the scalp. The EEG can be understood by analogy to the electrocardiogram, or EKG, which actually was discovered first. Here the electrical activity of the contracting heart muscle is picked up by an electrode pasted onto the skin with conductive paste. Inside the skin, the body is actually a good conductor, so the electrical fluctuations generated by the heart are easily observable at the skin. The same holds true for the electrical activity of the brain, only the signal is very much smaller.

The EEG reflects particular aspects of brain behavior, namely those concerned with regulating the brain itself. It is the nerve cells predominantly involved in organizing brain function whose electrical activity shows up in the EEG. The biofeedback process may be understood by analogy to a car mechanic listening to an engine. If the engine is badly tuned, the sound gives it away. And just as in earlier days the mechanic might well have tuned the engine by sound, the brain has a chance to be its own mechanic and tune itself just on the basis of seeing how well it is doing. All that is required for this process to occur is for the brain to be given the relevant information.

This is how the brain learns to behave in the world in general. The dancer learns to improve her motor skills by viewing herself in the mirror. The brain learns to improve its own behavior by watching its own EEG. It's really the same story. When the brain gets to see information derived from its own EEG, it quickly recognizes that the signal reflects its own efforts, and then it acts upon that information. The brain has lots of internal feedback on its activities already; now we find that providing external feedback can be helpful to the brain as well.

Unfortunately the EEG signal unfolding on the screen is not particularly meaningful to the person. And presenting the entire EEG signal back to the brain is not terribly helpful either. But by extracting certain EEG frequencies derived from specific cortical sites we give the brain more selective information that it can relate to more readily. By building in a challenge, we also have a better chance of retaining the person's engagement with the process. The expectation is that by giving the brain this information, and repeatedly confronting it with a challenge to change, it can in fact learn to change its vulnerability to seizures. This had been proved a number of years earlier in numerous studies, principally by Professor M. Barry Sterman of the UCLA School of Medicine, the original discoverer of the method.

The whole concept made sense to Sue, as it was explained to her by Margaret Ayers in their first phone conversation. Sue's graduate work in neurobiology was in fact related to this area of inquiry. Sue had implanted electrodes in a number of cats, and had trained them in an avoidance response. She was looking for changes in the EEG that were related to the newly learned behavior. This was yet another experiment in behavioral conditioning, so Sue felt very comfortable with the story Ayers was telling. Sue had initiated her experimental work at Cornell, and then brought her research animals to the UCLA Brain Research Institute when we came out in 1970. Ironically, Sue was doing this work at the very same time that Barry Sterman was conducting his critical neurofeedback research on seizure management at the nearby Sepulveda Veterans Administration Hospital.

Margaret Ayers' office was conveniently located nearby in Beverly Hills, and Sue set up an appointment for Brian. In the course of the conversation, Margaret asked Sue:

"Would you like to know the fee?"

As a matter of fact Sue did want to know, and she was relieved to hear that the fee was a reasonable $40 per session. But it would not have mattered one way or the other. We were clearly going to explore this new avenue with Brian regardless of cost in terms of time and money. This did not mean we weren't skeptical of what we were undertaking. Of course we were skeptical. We had already burned out on other initiatives, and our hopes at best were on a low flame. Nevertheless, we had an obligation to try anything that gave us some reasonable expectation of helping. Had we consulted a neurologist on this matter, we would surely have been warned off. We were very much on our own, as indeed were nearly all of Margaret Ayers' clients when we got to meet them.

# 2

# BRIAN AND HIS BRAIN

## FIRST TRAINING SESSION

On March 5, 1985 Brian had his first EEG training session. He was 16 years old, and in 11th grade at Highland Hall. His EEG showed more seizure-like activity on the left hemisphere, which is our logical, lexical, and analytical side. This is where the EEG training was begun, but not because that's where the seizure focus was. In this time frame nearly everyone was being trained on the left side of the brain. Some considerable inroads had been made in understanding left-hemisphere function, whereas the right hemisphere remained more of a mystery. Epilepsy tends to result in a lot of low-frequency activity in the EEG. The biofeedback instrument let Brian know—via a flashing red light—whenever his brainwaves got too large at low frequency. This indicated incipient loss of control, so in fact Brian's brain was constantly changing in its level of internal control. Sooner or later, the red light would go out again, and Brian would experience this as a small triumph in his venture of brain training. The training session would consist of a sequence of such little triumphs.

Brian was also shown how much brainwave activity there was in the region of 15 Hz (cycles per second), in the frequency band that had been identified by Sterman as playing a key role in quieting the motor system. The brain has pacemaker circuitry that regulates brain activity at various frequencies across the band. Neurons then have a propensity to fire rhythmically at the select frequencies. Some frequencies play special roles in special places, such as the well-known alpha frequency at around 10Hz, which ties into the quieting of the visual system. Increasing activity at 15Hz moves the brain toward greater quiescence of the motor system, which has beneficial fallout for brain stability in general. In any event, this exercise helps the brain do a better job of regulating its own activity.

The biofeedback instrument let Brian know how much 15-Hz activity was going on in his brain at any moment. This signal controlled the brightness of a little green light, and Brian would spend his half-hour session trying to keep the green light as bright as possible. When a threshold criterion was met, he would be rewarded with a beep. This beep could come along as frequently as twice a second. So in practice he would try to get as long a run of beeps as possible. And when the beeps stopped, he would ardently wish for them to start up again. This structuring of the process gave Brian the sense of consciously being in charge of the process, that all of this was his doing. The reality (we now understand) might well be quite something else. No one really knew then just how much difference one's voluntary engagement actually made. We know that it matters very little. At a minimum, however, it helped at the level of staying engaged with what was at that time a rather tedious and boring process.

## SIGNIFICANT CHANGES

Brian started training at two sessions per week, 30 minutes each. Significant changes started coming so quickly that Sue decided to keep a diary in order that the flow of events would not be obscured later by faulty memory. After just a few weeks of training, we had a chance to spend the weekend at Point Mugu State Park. It was the annual gathering of volunteer naturalists working in the Santa Monica Mountains. Sue was founder/director of one such group, the Topanga Canyon Docents, and had organized this annual gathering. At this event, friends who knew Brian thought he was "lighter." For our part, we noticed that we were no longer being treated to Brian's irrational outbursts. An episode in which Brian cut his hand with his wood-carving knife passed benignly.

Brian was simultaneously undergoing social skills training with Dr. Janice Peterson. She was helping the group improve conversational skills, and was taking them to restaurants to learn how to order, etc. Brian was now benefiting more from that opportunity. Sue recalls Brian talking on the phone to a friend and asking, "And how was your weekend?" That was a new departure indeed.

About one month after the training was begun, we took a trip to Monterey Bay to see the new aquarium. Brian did not want to go along, and I had long ago vowed never to undertake another lengthy trip with both children in the car. It was a formula for family crisis. But Sue was understandably unwilling to leave Brian behind with the house sitter. We undertook the trip with some misgivings. Forced to go along, Brian was intending to be a non-participant, withdrawing to his book. It did not happen. Repeatedly, he was drawn into the conversation despite himself. Once we looked back at Brian and Kurt in the backseat of the Vanagon Camper and found them asleep on each other's shoulder. Dare we believe it? Were we going to be allowed to enjoy parenting again?

## SUE'S JOURNAL

Some notes from Sue's journal starting one month into the process:

*April 7. Drive from Morro Bay to Monterey. Brian's good spirits continue to make this the best trip ever.*

*April 8. We all have a fantastic day at the aquarium.*

*April 12. Brian is coming out of his room in the evening to engage someone in conversation. He is hanging around after dinner to talk and socialize. He is smiling and laughing, and can even take a joke.*

*April 17. Brian is acknowledging changes in himself. He believes that he is concentrating better.*

Before this, when Sue had asked him whether he was aware of any changes in himself, Brian had said no, but he allowed that "Kurt is nicer to me now." In fact, of course, it was quite the other way around, and Kurt simply responded.

*April 18. Brian is carrying his medicine with him and remembering to take it by himself.*

*April 19. Brian reports that he thinks he should be right-handed. We talked about switching.*

By this time in his life, Brian is a confirmed left-handed writer. But he had suddenly developed the sense that neurologically he is really right-handed. It would take a period of training his right hand to take over the burdens of the left, and this was left to another day. Over time, Brian became exquisitely aware of issues related to hemispheric function, no doubt precisely because of the various ways in which each hemisphere was failing in its function.

*April 20. Brian is planning ahead. He is thinking about a summer job to earn money for his projects.*

*April 22. Brian spent the evening talking my ear off about school and about rock climbing.*

*April 23. Brian and Kurt are walking back from the school bus having conversations these days, instead of Kurt arriving alone in tears.*

*April 25. ...for the first time we are seriously considering Brian's going away to college...*

*April 26. Brian was irritable and unpleasant all afternoon and evening. He was at least aware that it was he who had the problem, and not everyone else.*

*April 30. Margaret says Brian is doing so well she would like to have him start reducing his medication.*

*May 3 (ninth week of training). Brian expects to finish his main lesson book—the first time ever. He expressed interest in going to parties again—for the first time since eighth grade.*

*May 21. Brian reports that note-taking and writing of main lesson books is getting easier.*

*For the first time, Brian is talking at length about changes he sees in himself: He can now think about the good things in life. He used to think and imagine and dream*

*about what he hated and what made him angry. He says
the medicine allowed him to control his behavior but not
his feelings.*

*May 27. Brian got an A, and the second highest score,
on a math test which most of the class flunked. He is
scheduling his time better now. He handed in an
overdue project. He used to just forget about things
that were overdue.*

Remarkable here is the matter-of-fact recitation of the fact that Brian got an A on his math test, in such contrast to his classmates. Was this not extraordinary? Of course it was, but Brian had all along given us glimpses of unusual abilities.

*May 28. Recorded Brian's EEG. Observed considerable
reduction in EEG amplitude and in incidence of low
frequency activity.*

Ayers had a clinical EEG system in her office, so that a clinical EEG could be obtained readily for a modest number of EEG channels.

*May 29. Saw Dr. Marshall. He thinks Brian is just
outgrowing his learning disabilities. It remains for him
to be convinced, but he is willing to reduce the Dilantin
dose (though not the Tegretol).*

*June 3. Marshall is willing to give this a chance if he can
dictate the changes in medication.*

*June 5. Reducing Dilantin from 300mg to 260mg per day.*

Yeah, people just routinely outgrow their learning disabilities! Dr. Marshall knew perfectly well that was unlikely, but what choice did he have when the alternative was to give credit to the neurofeedback?

The reduction in medication was begun exactly three months from the start of training, during which interval Brian had had some twenty-four training sessions.

> *June 9. Brian is much more responsive to Kurt. He doesn't always shut him up with "I don't want to know" or "I don't care." Kurt built his Lego train into a message delivery system in his cardboard fort. He sent Brian a message: "I love you." Brian returned with "I love you too but I have work to do so bye."*

> *We have come a long way from "Brian is lion, and Kirt is dirt."*

> *June 19. Reducing Dilantin level from 260mg to 230mg per day. Marshall thought it might take a year to get Brian drug-free. Margaret also talked in terms of a year.*

> *June 28. Saw Dr. Marshall for the first time since reducing Dilantin. Brian was the model of decorum. Dr. Marshall showed signs of being persuadable. He asked about the changes in the EEG that we had seen.*

> *July 1. Marshall says Dilantin blood level is barely measurable. OK'd a decrease of another 30mg to 200mg per day.*

> *Interruption of training through July for trip to the Golden Trout Wilderness, and for Brian's Sierra backpack.*

The trip to the Golden Trout Wilderness in the Sierra Nevadas Southwest of Lone Pine was memorable for several reasons. We were staying at the Audubon Camp with an Audubon group. We all undertook joint outings during the day. But one day, Brian headed off on his own to Mount Langley, some seven miles away, and with perhaps 4,000 feet of altitude gain to above 14,000 feet. He took off after breakfast, and returned in time for high tea. It had been quite an undertaking. Brian conveyed to us how it was done: "You just don't stop," he said, in perfect seriousness. He also decided to go fairly directly, cross-country, thus cutting off some switch-backs. Actually, he had lost the trail, and just headed directly for Army Pass.

On that same trip, however, Brian had an episode in which he became extremely enraged. The cause is lost to memory. He was so angry that we were afraid that he might hit us. He was now my size, and incredibly strong. He must have seen the fear in our eyes, because he came back later, after he had calmed down, to say that regardless of how angry he became, he would never hit his parents. I was touched, but not reassured. I was sure only that if he ever did hit one of us, he would be very remorseful afterwards. In fact, it never came close again to violence. The EEG biofeedback had come along just in time.

> *July 29. Decreased Dilantin to 160mg—below the therapeutic range. We can therefore count on being able to reduce it to zero over time.*

> *August 3. Brian said it was hard for him to remember just how bad it was before he started the EEG biofeedback training.*

> *September 4. Decreased Dilantin dose to 130mg per day.*

> *September 18. Decreased Dilantin dose to 100mg per day.*

> *September 28. Brian asked for an appointment calendar to keep track of his assignments. (We had bought him calendars for years, but he never used them previously.) He is slowly gaining control over more and more of his life.*

*September 29. Brian is incorporating regular exercise and clarinet practice into his schedule.*

*October 5. Dr. Marshall was impressed with Brian's improvement. It has been 27 weeks of training so far, or about 54 sessions.*

*October 16. Dilantin level reduced to 30mg per day.*

*October 19. Brian has much more energy after reducing Dilantin dose. He is joining the school cross-country team.*

*October 30. Dilantin level reduced to zero! It has been 61 sessions.*

*November 5. Brian complemented Margaret on her clothes!*

*November 8. Brian enthusiastically and on his own initiative bought a watch for Kurt's birthday.*

*Such interest in someone else's desires and happiness is a welcome change.*

*November 9. Brian ran in 5K race.*

*November 11. Brian began reducing Tegretol level, from 1000 to 950mg.*

*November 19. Spiking activity still evident in the EEG.*

*December 10. Tegretol level to 900mg.*

*December 27. Tegretol level to 850mg.*

## PARENTAL SKEPTICISM

Sue's journal stops at year-end. By this time it was perfectly clear that the biofeedback training was helping in all of the crucial areas. We had not been misled by wishful thinking or gauzy memory. The journal had served its purpose. In actual fact, one's desire to see positive change with any new undertaking also causes one to be his own skeptic. This is not generally understood. "Desperate parents" are thought to be willing to clutch any glimmer of progress and perhaps even imagine progress where there is none. More likely the opposite is the case. Parents are progressively humbled by one failed undertaking after another, and their skepticism is sharpened.

When we began to see changes in Brian initially, we were trying very hard not to be swayed by them. Sue and I saw these changes independently, but we didn't mention them to each other, and didn't confer on them, for some weeks. The most important force at work here is that you don't want to set yourself up for disappointment later. Not to believe the positive changes when they are first observed serves to protect your own vulnerable psyche. "Don't get your hopes up," as they say. It is noteworthy in this regard that the first real acknowledgement of positive change that Sue committed to the diary was what other people observed about Brian. Somehow that was taken to be more objective evidence. After all, they did not know that Brian was undergoing the EEG training. Their testimony was like a "blind test," in scientists' parlance. And only after that event had occurred did we start sharing our own observations with each other.

It has been pointed out that parents who have a disabled child undergo a grieving process, much as for a child that they have lost. It is helpful to have that understanding. We grieve the death of a dream, the dream we have for our child. This is an enduring process that involves one's whole being and colors all of one's experience. It is not undone suddenly even with some welcome news. It takes a lot of evidence, and a lot of time, to emerge out of that emotional pit. The process is like a roller-coaster ride of highs and lows. So you temper your judgments in order not to experience emotional whiplash along the way.

## THE LEARNING CURVE

Despite the favorable changes we were seeing, Brian was still having severe problems. By the end of 1985 we were unambiguously convinced that the EEG biofeedback had enabled Brian to control his behavior in a significant way. The changes were too profound and too comprehensive to be dismissed. We had witnessed fairly systematic progress—a learning curve, if you will—along a number of dimensions of functioning. There was the subsidence of the rage behavior, first of all. There were the improvements in communication skills at so many levels, in particular the basic issue of relating to other people. Most prominently, there were the improvements in the relationship to Kurt. There were the improvements in planning and time management. Brian's academics improved by leaps and bounds to the point where going on to college became a realistic possibility.

For the first time in years, Brian could see interaction with other people as a positive experience. He was practically giddy with excitement about having friends again. Instead of taking off into the chaparral after school he would now plop his body down at the kitchen table after school and engage Sue in what she called his "conversation fix." He had a lot to catch up on.

On the downside, however, it was clear that his behavioral control could still go off the rails. We were seeing higher highs and less severe lows, but the fluctuations were still there, and loss of control was still a risk. Consequently we still maintained our habits of vigilance and chose our words carefully when dealing with Brian.

## THE PLACEBO EFFECT?

The improvements in Brian's overall comportment were accompanied by partial normalization of Brian's bizarre EEG, and they were not undone by a decrease in Brian's medication dose. An independent, objective scientist might still wonder if the progress Brian made was due to the positive expectations that were created in him with all of the fancy machinery and loving attention that was being showered on him in this connection—the infamous placebo effect. The part of you that is parent really doesn't care, of course. We'll take progress any way we can get it. The scientist part of you would like to know, however, how much of the change is "objectively" produced (by the EEG biofeedback), and which is subjectively produced (by engaging in a process in a supportive, hopeful environment).

Whereas the question may always be on our minds as scientists, it may ultimately have no satisfactory resolution in any particular case. It is impossible to tease these elements apart in any one individual. The medical doctor, too, uses the subjective dimension of the healing arts to his advantage. He comes at you with the status-defining white coat, tells you that you will be all right in an authoritative voice, charges you a lot of money, and is not above giving you a sugar pill if he has nothing better. At its best, medicine also wants to invoke all the elements that can promote recovery, even the "subjective" ones. In the case of biofeed-back, the intermingling of the subjective dimension with the objective is intrinsic to the process.

By virtue of this inseparability of the subjective and the objective dimension in biofeedback, it follows that we can prove nothing "objective" with a single case. With Brian certainly the subjective dimension was quite significant. The biofeedback training gave him a strong sense of empowerment. Here finally was something he could do for himself to master his condition. Up to that time, he had suffered a pervasive sense of victimization. His brain was unreliable. His doctor told him that this was a lifetime condition, and that medication was the only thing that could help. The medication, however, afforded only a partial remedy. And then there were the side effects. All the problems the medication did not address Brian feared he might not overcome. His parents were down on him all the time. Friends were fickle. He really didn't have any. Brian saw himself a failure in so many ways. And yet he was trying so hard! Life really was unfair. The biofeedback opened a window of opportunity for him, and he grasped it firmly.

## PARENTAL BURDEN

The sense of victimization, of course, extends to the parents as well, if truth be told. I expect that one of these days a book will be published titled *Parent Abuse*. I could certainly contribute a chapter. Children think nothing of placing unbounded demands on their parents. Brian's condition, and his suffering, rendered him even more self-absorbed than other children. The demands he made on us as parents took us to the limits of our ability.

On the one hand, there is a larger burden on the parents of a disabled child. And on the other, there is such a meager payoff for all that effort. The result is psychic exhaustion. The reservoir of emotional resources gets depleted. It is a combination of the relentlessness and the hopelessness of the challenge. Viewed in that frame, Sue's almost unbounded patience and forbearance in managing Brian was remarkable. Sue had been bearing the main burden of parenting throughout Brian's life. Over much of this time I was off working at my job in aerospace, leaving early in the morning and coming home late in the evening in order to avoid the peak of LA traffic. Mine was the usual urban dumbbell life—a lump at one end and a lump at the other, with a freeway in between.

But everyone has limits. Kurt relates that his greatest moments of terror were when Sue would capitulate and insist that he and Brian sort their altercation out for themselves. At those times, Kurt saw himself completely at Brian's mercy. And on one occasion, Sue had been so totally exasperated with Brian that she told him to get out of the car and walk home. At that instant, you don't want him in your sight. Does that mean you don't love your child? On the contrary, because of the rejection of him by the rest of the world, you compensate with your own generous emotional embrace. This does not mean, however, that you don't occasionally bang against the stops and have nothing left for him.

It must also be said that asking Brian to walk home was not really as neglectful as it might seem. Brian always had an uncanny sense of direction. It would have been quite impossible to lose him. The only time I recall when Brian couldn't find his way back was while camping at Indian Cove in Joshua Tree National Monument. Brian had hiked into Rattlesnake Canyon on his own, and a kind fellow offered him a ride back in his truck. The road took Brian away from his landmarks, and so he was unable to direct the person back to our campsite. It took quite a while for him to locate us. On this occasion, he was truly lost.

One of the demands placed on us by our children is to be perfect parents. Any shortcoming is immediately thrust back in our face. And you have to take this from such an imperfect child? With all his deficits, Brian remains an exquisite detector of imperfect parenting. One of the lessons we had to learn over the years is what we could genuinely hold him responsible for, and what was beyond his control. Often the distinction was not that apparent. Acts that appeared to be volitional were in fact neurologically driven.

This came home to me early on in an episode I am embarrassed to recall, but is an essential part of the story. Brian had a bad case of runny nose, and he was never near either a handkerchief or a Kleenex. He did what came naturally, which was to suck up air through his nose and retain the mucus in perpetual suspension. As this snurfing became more frequent, I progressively pegged out.

"Blow your nose, Brian!"

Snurf.

"Blow your nose, Brian!"

Snurf.

"BLOW YOUR NOSE, BRIAN!"

SNURF.

"Get a Kleenex and blow your nose, Brian."

Snurf.

I brought him a Kleenex.

Snurf.

I held it under his nose.

Snurf.

"Blow out, not in, Brian."

Snurf.

"OUT, Brian. Not in."

Snurf.

The legacy of my fatherly upbringing was taking over. I was going to have my way with this obstreperous child if it took me all evening. Surely he could understand such a simple instruction, and this is merely a case of intolerable stubbornness. I had not chosen the time or the battleground, but if this was the time, and this the place, then so be it.

The back and forth continued. I gave him time to comply. I reasoned with him. I thundered. I cajoled. I threatened. I promised. We reduced the issue to its simplest essence: *Out, not in!* By this time, Brian was a whimpering lump sitting on the floor in the hallway, saying nothing, but occasionally snurfing. I finally managed to rise above the situation and realize that this was not a child engaging in a dominance battle with his father. This was a child whose brain was caught in a kind of loop from which he could not voluntarily escape, much like a software subroutine that once it is finished goes back to the beginning and starts over again. In the case of the computer, you can do "Ctrl-Alt-Del" and start all over again. But in Brian's case, he would have to get out of the loop on his own. I was only making it worse. I was the command that simply re-initialized the subroutine.

It was a difficult lesson to learn. Brian was conscious; he was processing what I was saying. But he could not voluntarily act as he would wish! This was similar to what was going on with his violent episodes. Some part of his brain took over and he did things that he later regretted, and over which he had no control at the time. For his own self-preservation, he had to learn to distinguish between "self" and the "non self" that was doing things he did not wish to do. The diagnosis of temporal lobe epilepsy first gave him permission to make that distinction. It was his brain that was causing all the trouble, not he himself. We also had to learn to make that distinction, so that we did not blame him for things that were not under his control. Since there was often a seamless transition from controlled to uncontrolled behavior, this was something we could only learn over time. At least we now had a framework in which to understand our son.

To understand your son is also to forgive him. As we learned that we could not blame him for the quirkiness and instability of his brain, for his genes, and for what fate dealt him, we also realized that the same thing held for us as parents. Whereas Brian demanded of us that we be perfect parents, we learned to accept that we weren't going to be perfect, and that doing our best was going to have to be good enough.

The biofeedback training and its positive effect on Brian only served to confirm for both Brian and us that we were dealing with neurologically based phenomena. We learned to talk matter-of-factly about what we were observing from both the inside and the outside. This objectification of the problem was enormously helpful in dissipating the emotional baggage associated with such discussions. It gets the question of blame off the table, and makes for a mutuality of concern and of interest, as opposed to making it an issue of us versus him. By the same token, this attitude also helps when confronting one's own issues.

## IMPROVEMENTS

Brian continued the EEG training with regularity, and the positive changes accumulated. He became more conversational. He became friendly to others, and actively sought out their company. He organized his school work. His grades came up. He was finishing his work. The decline in his medication dose also continued, and this had further benefits in terms of mental quickness and alertness. The dulling of his eyes disappeared. He seemed more alive, more present.

The Tegretol level was reduced slowly, as had been the case with Dilantin. However, in this instance Dr. Marshall became much more cautious.

"Before I agree to any more reduction in medication, I want you to get an EEG."

"We are getting an EEG twice a week," said Sue.

"No. I want a real EEG!"

We made an appointment with Dr. Pellegrino, a neurologist conveniently housed in the same building, for the EEG. When Sue met with Dr. Pellegrino to review the results, he declared with finality:

"This child does not have temporal lobe epilepsy, and never did."

In our desire to persuade him that Brian did indeed have such problems, we almost failed to notice that we had gotten what we came for. Clearly, he would tell Dr. Marshall that it was okay to reduce the Tegretol level! Since Brian did not have temporal lobe epilepsy, there was no need for the Tegretol at all. We did enjoy the irony. Within the space of a single week, the pediatrician wrings his hands about reducing medication levels, and the neurologist declares there never was a problem in the first place. The reduction in Tegretol proceeded:

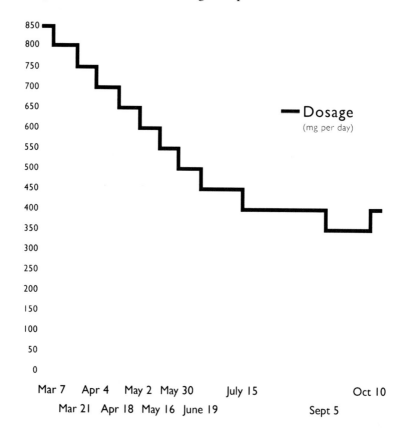

By September/October we had found the level of medication that Brian needed at this time to maintain adequate behavioral control. Over the next few years, this level would fluctuate, with a pattern of initial increase because of Brian's greater weight and activity level, and subsequently of general decline over the years down to a level of about 125mg. A neurologist is likely to say that 125mg is too far below the therapeutically effective dose (about 300mg) to be an issue at all. Not so! Brian came to know himself so well that he could tell the difference between having 100mg or 125mg on a particular day. More than that, he found it advantageous to divide even this small dose into several portions so that the effect would not be too concentrated. Should one necessarily believe the judgments of an authority figure, or should one believe the careful observations of the person who has learned to monitor himself? To us, averages over populations could not decide the issue. We came to know what was true for Brian, but first Brian came to know what was true for himself. It took us some time to have the courage to disagree with the "ex cathedra" pronouncements of learned neurologists. But in the end the evidence spoke louder than doctrine. Brian was already there.

## SELF-MONITORING

The next stage in Brian's EEG biofeedback training in fact involved a growth in self-monitoring. Since his brain was still not self-regulating properly, he had to complement it on the conscious level. The issues were more complex than one of either more or less medication.

It became obvious that the quality of Brian's sleep had a great deal to do with how he did the next day. So a priority had to be given to scheduling sleep. Brian could not simply work into the night to finish a project without paying a huge price the next day. Over time, Brian developed an extraordinary awareness around his own sleep patterns.

Then there was the issue of diet. We came to realize that Brian was extremely sensitive to paprika and allspice. Spices are of course selected for their ability to stimulate the nervous system. That's the whole point. For those whose nervous systems are potentially unstable, spices may be a particular hazard. Brian had to avoid chocolate as well. Fortunately he didn't have much of a sweet tooth. Occasionally he would sample chocolate substitutes like carob.

So while the biofeedback training continued aggressively, it was no longer a clear-cut issue as to what was being contributed by the training per se to Brian's improved functionality. It did not really matter in the final analysis. The biofeedback had set him out on a voyage of discovery with respect to his own nervous system, one that was now multi-faceted. The training continued to give him improved stability, allowing him to experience higher levels of mental performance and also allowing him to experience pleasure in being in his own company, which some of us take for granted. Once such higher plateaus of performance are experienced, the falls from those heights, whether produced by dietary indiscretions, by lack of sleep, or by failure to take the medication, are progressively less acceptable. So the various aspects of his course of remediation, involving not only biofeedback, sleep and diet, but also exercise and attention to breathing, and the proper dose of medication, were mutually reinforcing.

## ACADEMICS

Brian's academic performance continued to improve, so much so that by spring of 1986 we looked into the possibility of his going to college. California Lutheran University offered the "Plus Program," by which students who were marginal academically but yet showed promise could gain admittance on a provisional basis. We took Brian there for an interview, and explained his history. He was accepted into the Plus Program, and the staff took great care to prepare him psychologically for the possibility of failure. Cal Lutheran was close by, in Thousand Oaks, allowing Brian to continue his EEG training on a weekly basis. By the time he entered college he'd had well over 100 neurofeedback sessions. Cal Lutheran was also small enough for the faculty to take a personal interest in the students. In fact, freshmen were each invited to be part of a small social group in which a member of the faculty or staff participated. This eased the entry into the impersonal life of the university.

When Brian registered for his first semester in the fall, he was given a recommended set of courses. Because of his marginal academic status, they loaded him up with soft social studies courses. This was of course a mistake. Those are the areas where he would have the greatest difficulty. We recognized this, and changed his program to be heavy in math and the physical sciences, which we were sure he would master. He chose a computer science major. By the end of the first year, he was in fact near the top of his class in that curriculum.

## BRIAN'S JOURNAL

When he started college, Brian also decided to keep a journal of his continuing preoccupation with his brain. This project got started when he was asked to write a brief autobiography in his first semester. He simply continued writing in diary format. During this time, we saw less and less of him, with the exception of the weekly trip to Beverly Hills to obtain his EEG training sessions. Our role changed more to being cheerleaders on the sidelines, so it is entirely appropriate that in telling the rest of the story we allow Brian to take the lead.

It is very clear from his journal that it was intended for his eyes only, and in his abiding attempt to understand himself the diary shows him in his good form as well as in his moments of utter despair and near derangement. In parts, it is painful for a parent to read.

## THE CLEAN WINDSHIELD EFFECT

Before turning to Brian's diary there are a couple of other threads to the story which must be picked up. Once Brian began to benefit so obviously from his EEG biofeedback sessions we were encouraged to try the training ourselves. Sue, for example, had been suffering for years from hypoglycemia, a disregulation of glucose blood level. It sapped her energy level, and she was frequently ill before this issue was identified. Years earlier, Sue's energy level had been so low that she was forced to abandon the dissertation work for her Ph.D., even though it was near completion. The death of her major advisor at Cornell had made it difficult to continue in any event. UCLA was unwilling to transfer her credits. Nevertheless, Sue continued for a time with her research at the UCLA Brain Research Institute, under the supervision of its Director, Professor Ross Adey. Eventually, her hypoglycemia made it impossible for her to continue.

Sue assumed that the termination of her degree program meant the end of her career in neurobiology, so she donated all of her technical library to UCLA, and her experimental cats to other research. The documentary residue from her dissertation project, consisting largely of stacks of Z-fold paper with EEG recordings, ended up in storage in our garage, where termites later took possession of them for their living quarters.

But back to the story. A glucose tolerance test was administered in order to rule out diabetes as the cause of Sue's frequent infections. The doctor did not take as significant that after consumption of the glucola, Sue was practically unable to move because her blood sugar level was now dangerously low. She had been told to come back in a few hours for the blood tests, yet she didn't have the energy to get up off the couch in the waiting room. Sue took this as significant, even if the doctor did not. With the aid of medical student friends, she began to research the issue, but to no avail. In those days, hypoglycemia was not a concept within the field of medicine.

Sue continued to suffer with this condition for some years until she came across the book *Low Blood Sugar and You*, by Carlton Fredericks. It was a Godsend. There Sue saw herself described within the first few pages. The remedy was to be found in controlling her diet. Consumption of sugar, or foods readily convertible to sugar, causes first a sharp rise, and then a compensatory large drop in glucose level that has adverse consequences for energy level and mental functioning over several hours. If one eliminated such a sugar challenge to the system, then such wild excursions could be avoided. This Sue had already been doing, to good effect, when Margaret Ayers suggested she try the EEG biofeedback training. When I came home from work the evening after her first session, Sue announced that there was a new person in the house. Only after checking out the living room, etc., in puzzlement, did the grin on her face disclose that she was referring to herself.

Sue had experienced what we later came to call the "clean windshield effect," a new mental clarity and greater energy level. Others have described it as "cleaning out the cobwebs of the brain." After many sessions, conducted over the fall of 85 and spring of 86, Sue was able to relax her dietary constraints and function more effectively as well.

## HYPERACTIVITY

Kurt had been very hyperactive in school, and in social situations. Some years previously, when he was about four years old, he went out trick-or-treating on Halloween for the first time, costumed in a little policeman's uniform and moustache. By the time he came back, he was a "space cadet." He was totally wired, with fire in his eyes. He bounced off the walls, and was totally unmanageable. He had discovered food, and it was called "sugar." Sue was running a low-sugar household at the time because of her own hypoglycemia. So in the ordinary course of events Kurt was not exposed to sweets. At Halloween, he had gotten an inadvertent glucose tolerance test. And he had failed.

It was difficult to persuade Kurt at his age that his newly discovered food was not in his own best interest. But we prevailed. Now in 1985, with Kurt nearly ten years old, we had a chance to try the EEG training with him. It had the expected effects. Over time, his hyperactive behavior normalized, and his dietary constraints could be relaxed as well.

## VERTIGO

And then there was me. On the camping trip with Brian's seventh grade to Yosemite back in 1981, I had imprudently participated with the kids in a game of jumping over a pile of tires. I ended up coming down on my head and neck, suffering a whiplash injury in the bargain. The next day I could not stay awake driving, so I had to turn the job over to another staff member. I had also become much more irritable, and I experienced periods of vertigo that kept me away from my job for days at a time. Gradually, these symptoms diminished by themselves, as they commonly do in minor head injury. However, there were still the occasional bouts of vertigo. At a more subtle level, I was also observing moments at which I could not play back in my mind what I had just said, and in consequence I would then have to repeat myself. Now in 1985, Ayers identified small spikes in my EEG that are commonly associated with head injury. These were eliminated within a few EEG training sessions, and what remained of my irritability appeared to melt away. There were no further episodes of vertigo, and there were no more episodes of memory holes.

## A NEW SYSTEM

So we all had our own personal experiences with the EEG training. This helped to persuade us of the general applicability of the technique. In each case, Margaret had led us to expect the recoveries that we then experienced personally. In addition, Sue also witnessed the comings and goings at Margaret's office while she was sitting in the waiting room. In one very dramatic instance, she witnessed the recovery of a man who had been injured in a horseback riding accident. He had lost the power of speech, and he suffered from amnesia. Since Margaret expected success, the man's wife was bringing along a tape recorder to document progress. When the man recovered speech over just a few sessions, his first words to his wife were to "shut that damn thing off." Everyone was thrilled. Initially he had been brought to the office in a straitjacket because he could suddenly fly into a rage. After a few sessions, his daughter brought him in for the first time, and he had told her how to get there. There was no more need for a straitjacket.

Another case was that of a Pakistani girl who suffered amnesia as a result of the loss of oxygen during surgery. She was in a wheelchair, not having any control of her limbs, and she could not speak. All other therapies had been terminated. Her professional parents sought additional help from around the world, and had found their way to Margaret's office. After a lengthy period of training, the girl was again able to converse with her sister in Pakistan in the secret language they had developed between them. She was now getting around on crutches. Astounding.

We came to this technique with our respective professional backgrounds—Sue's in neurobiology, and mine in physics and engineering. With all of these experiences with the technique, we were increasingly motivated to get involved in bringing the instrumentation up to date technically, and in making it more broadly available. Sue and I were both prepared to change our careers to do this, if it came to that. If all we were able to do was to help more people like our son Brian, that would already be enough. But what we had witnessed implied a much larger potential role for EEG biofeedback. At this moment, however, the horizon was more limited. The immediate opportunity lay in modernizing the instrumentation by converting a hardware-based system into a computerized one. That would allow for much more design flexibility, for future growth, and for integration with video feedback. And it would allow us to display the EEG signal so that clinicians would always have it available to look at.

Within a few months of beginning Brian's training, I approached Margaret Ayers with an offer to develop a new system for her entirely at our risk. If she liked it, then we would arrange to go into business together to build up a professional community around it. If she didn't like it, then that would be our problem. Margaret was surprisingly reluctant at first. She was used to working independently. She saw her existing instrument as the key to her uniqueness, which she greatly valued. Once a new instrument was built, there would not be just one. There had also been so much hostility to her work that she had become very wary. Indeed we were not the first ones to have come along with an offer of help.

But eventually she agreed. A three-way partnership was formed between Ayers, myself, and the software engineer I had recruited to the task, Edward Dillingham. Our partnership was sealed over a meal at the original Cheesecake Factory in Beverly Hills in the fall of 1985. We then went back to Margaret's office and she invited us into a mutual ceremonial hug. For the first time, Margaret appeared to relish the moment. It was an auspicious and hopeful beginning. Brian had been training for about six months, and the rest of us had benefited from the training as well. Ed then committed what turned out to be nearly three years to the software development task—all without pay.

# 3

## CAL LUTHERAN
### FALL 1986-SUMMER 1988

Brian confidently trucked off to Cal Lutheran in Thousand Oaks in the fall of 1986. At this small university emphasis is placed on per- sonal connections with faculty and staff. We thought he was in good hands there. With many of the bounds on his freedom removed, he now needed to make his way in a new environment. Early in his college career, he was asked to write an essay about his own life. This essay then morphed into his journal. The following are excerpts.

## HALLOWEEN

*It is Halloween night. Tonight I saw several movies. How I feel after these movies is worth recording. I saw a movie,* Rocky 3, *in which two people, both very strong boxers, let their heads get treated like punching bags in order to win the fight. I was watching their faces get all bloody and deformed.* Then I saw Friday the Thirteenth, Part Three, *where I saw the bloody slaughter of 13 people with a machete, axe, knife, or blowgun. At ten p.m. I started watching another movie,* An American Werewolf in London. *In this movie I saw people drastically deformed into a werewolf.*

*All these movies made me feel so lucky and thankful that my body is not deformed, damaged, or mutilated. But I feel as if something has control over me right now. I feel not only lucky to be "still in one piece," but also feel that I want to destroy other things. I feel that my present emotion and appearance may make people mistake me for a drunk. I could easily lose control of my emotions right now. I feel like I'm in a trance, or that some other mysterious being is in control of my thoughts and emotions, but I am trying to keep control of my actions while this is happening.*

*I am here alone. If others were here and afflicting me, that could mean trouble.*

Brian's journal [Saturday, Halloween night, 11/1/86, 1:45 a.m.]

This entry dates to Brian's first year in college. It's been one-and-a-half years since he began training with neurofeedback. He is still quite vulnerable, but also curious about the propensity to violence that had taken strange control of his life. In a larger frame, he was vitally interested in the problem of good and evil.

The discussions of the effects of movies on violent behavior rarely focus specifically on those who are in fact potentially violent. Here is poignant evidence that those who are vulnerable are profoundly affected. Moreover, they are drawn to such movies. Brian feels the need to explore the part of himself that is potentially violent.

This is an area where perhaps the apple did not fall far away from the tree. My own reaction to movies is that I tend to be totally captivated by them and drawn into the experiences being portrayed. I cannot distance myself from them. As a result, there are a lot of movies that I cannot watch as a matter of both self-preservation and just plain mental hygiene. But this attitude took shape over many years. In one's teenage years the hunger for experience is such that deliberate distancing is unlikely. Brian's experience of movies may have been similarly absorbing. In that event, his ability to witness such violent imagery and walk away with equanimity is remarkable. But who knows what might have happened if he had been challenged at that moment?

From all indications, Brian's first year in college was a success. Brian spent the summer months of 1987 with us at home, learning to program a Commodore Amiga computer. He also took an art class. He had made his own choices, so he was drawn to his areas of strength. One was the world of math and computer science. Here Brian engaged with a rule-driven world, where it was a simple matter of learning the rules and the underlying principles. No sweat. Then there was the realm of the arts, where Brian turned out to be surprisingly gifted in some areas. During this summer he took an art class, where he came to be very absorbed in painting. Brian had an uncanny spatial sense, which found expression in two ways in particular. He was able to manipulate a 4x4 Rubics cube with such speed and finesse that the thing practically smoked. And in wood-working class in high school he had set himself the task of carving a sphere inside of a cage—out of a single piece of wood! As I survey the sphere now, I am unable to tell any

deviation from sphericity. Billiard balls must be spherical to a tolerance of one part in a thousand. Brian's carved ball may well come close. The symbolism is inescapable. One sees Pythagorean spherical perfection constructed inside a cage and then constrained by it.

Brian's third major area of interest was nature and the outdoors. Nature might be mysterious and unpredictable, and even appear capricious, but it is not malign. In pursuit of this interest, Brian took a trip to the Sierra Nevadas with the peak baggers, the serious mountain climbers of the Angeles Chapter of the Sierra Club. Brian originally had been told he shouldn't climb to high altitude because of his epilepsy. He almost took that as a challenge. He had been going on group trips to the high Sierras for a number of years, gradually increasing in difficulty. Here was his most daunting trip. Past trips had gone well, so we were not concerned. We left it to Brian to communicate to the others whatever he wanted them to know about his condition.

# BACKPACKING

*It is the second day of a nine-day backpacking trip with the Sierra Club. This is my very first trip with the Sierra Club, besides my trips with the Natural Science Section. I decided for once I would try and keep a journal, even though writing is not my strength.*

*Everyone on the trip is at least a decade older than me; most are twice my age; yet all of them are very strong and endured the 16-mile 5,700 foot climb better than I. With nine days' worth of food on my back, adding up to 60 pounds, hiking over alpine meadows and lakes was not easy.*

*During the morning of the first day I had hiked up from Mineral King Parking Lot to Glacier Pass, and down to Spring Lake to have lunch. We had started off at 7 a.m., and by the time we arrived at Spring Lake it was 1 p.m. We had climbed 3,000 ft., and descended 1,000 ft. I started to realize that carrying 60 pounds is not anywhere near the same as carrying 55 pounds. On the other hand, 45 pounds is not that much different from 40. So as a pack gets heavier, every pound added makes a bigger difference than the last.*

*Everyone on this trip, besides being in their 40s or 50s, is also more experienced and bar-barian than I. The lady who gave me a ride up did not bring more than one pair of underwear— the one she was wearing. Today as I lay here recuperating, one of the old mountaineers says, "Showers are superfluous, and a waste of time."*

*In response I said, "Don't you at least like to take one at the end of a trip?"*

*"No, they are totally superfluous," he said.*

*Many of these people did not bring many clothes to change into, only clothes to stay warm.*

*After lunch the first day, we headed cross-coun-try over lakes to reach a trail which climbed 2,500 feet to Black Rock Pass, approximately 11,700 feet in elevation. Around four-thirty we started to descend towards the Big Arroyo. I did not arrive there until 9 p.m., in the dark. I nibbled some gorp and went straight to bed around 9:25 p.m.*

Brian's journal [August 16, 1987, Sunday]

---

*Everything is beginning to get easier. My pack does not seem much lighter, but I am in much better shape. With a day of rest on the 16th for my muscles to heal, and a challenging climb on the 17th of Black Kaweah, I am beginning to feel more at home.*

*The trip up Black Kaweah was an all-day trip, primarily because we were a group of ten people. Had it been only a group of four, we could have climbed it twice as fast. More than half the day was spent climbing the last 1,300 feet, which was where we needed our helmets. Most of the time on this dangerous chute was spent waiting for other people to get out of someone's fall-line so that that person could move. This meant that people were always starting on one side or the other of the chute and every so often a few people would cross to the other side of the chute.*

*I had slept very well on the night of the 17th. I was all unorganized, though. I had planned to get organized after climbing Black Kaweah, but I had gotten back too late. After having a breakfast of oatmeal and hash browns, I started to get myself more organized, and packed.*

*I had gotten up at 6:20 a.m., and it was not yet 7:00 a.m. I had one hour to get organized. We were all supposed to aim for 7:30 a.m., but if it took us until 8:00 a.m. to be ready, the leader would understand. People were heading off on the trail by 7:50 a.m., and I was not ready.*

*We were hiking from the Big Arroyo (our base camp) to the highest lake in the Nine Lakes Basin, and we cut off-trail a little before passing Kaweah Gap on our left. It was only about five miles to this lake, and people who wanted a lay-over day and were not up to going over Pants Pass could stay here and make camp for the next two (or three) nights. Four people decided to stay at the lake. The other six people, including both leaders, continued.*

*We climbed over Pants Pass and down the other side. We had been told by a ranger that there was some class three, but it was all class two, with a lot of scree. Several of us chose not to climb Kern Point, for we knew we would be walking over lakes in the dark, and we would rather sit back and relax considering how little chance we get to do that. But the leaders are so devoted to climbing the peaks that they still go even if no one else wants to.*

Brian's journal, [August 18, 1987, Tuesday]

---

*I just arrived at the Big Arroyo again at a campsite near to the one we camped at before. It is much warmer down at the Big Arroyo than at Nine Lakes Basin, but there are also many more mosquitoes.*

*The last two days have been very strenuous. The leaders underestimated what was involved in going over Colby Pass, up Whale Back, around*

*Whale Back, and up over two passes, past Lion Lake, and back to the rest of the group.*

*We did not climb Whale Back, but went around the other side of it, in Cloud Canyon. We still all ended up having to bivouac. Two people in the group said they could make it all the way back to camp, and went on ahead of the rest of us. But they ended up camping only a quarter mile upstream. The two that went ahead were to tell the rest of the group in Nine Lakes Basin to meet us at the pass between Cloud Canyon and Lion Lake. From there we would climb Triple Divide Peak. It wasn't until the afternoon that people finally arrived from Nine Lakes Basin. They had brought a lot of food for us because they heard we were out of food and had nothing to eat. Half an hour later we started climbing Triple Divide Peak. We tried also to climb Lion Rock on the other side of Lion Lake, but were unsuccessful because it was too late and getting dark. I arrived back at camp in Nine Lakes Basin at 8:00 p.m. I went straight to bed. I also forgot my medicine and did not sleep well.*

*The next day (the 21st), I was first down the mountain, and first to start hiking to the Big Arroyo. I arrived at the Big Arroyo by 6:50 p.m., and the other four arrived fifty minutes later.*

Brian's journal [August 21, 1987, Friday]

*On the twenty-second, I impressed the leaders for the first time, by being packed and ready to go on time. One of the leaders said, "You finally got your act together, Brian. I'm impressed."*

*For lunch I started to eat my smoked gouda in huge pieces since tomorrow would be the last day. I passed out some of my sardines and my crackers. We ended up camping at only the third lake of the "Little Five Lakes." At 4:30 p.m. we were off to climb Mount Eisen. We did not make it. Even though we did not get to the summit, we still ended up coming back in the dark. I went straight to bed, and had only a glass of Milk Man (one quart).*

*Now the 23rd of August, I lay in bed feeling great but unwilling to get out into the cold air. We were at 10,000 feet elevation, and it was 6:00 a.m. At 6:20 a.m. I got out of bed and made myself some hot water to add to my oatmeal. I was the last one packed, and left about seven minutes after the leader (he was second to last to leave).*

*As we drove back to Sherman Oaks I rested in the back seat of the Blazer. They dropped me off at home. It was midnight. My father was working on the IBM, and came out to see what was happening. The dogs were inside sleeping, but soon they were racing out to see me.*

*After everything was inside, I told Sue about how strenuous my trip had been for about half an hour. Then Siegfried was about done with the computer, and we all went to bed.*

*Well, I have been home from my trip now for three days. I finally feel recovered and feel like writing in my journal.*

Brian's journal [August 26, 1987, Wednesday]

Brian told his diary a lot more about the trip than he told us. All had gone well healthwise, and Brian seemed to get along with everyone. This was undoubtedly helped by the large age gap between him and the rest of the group. We were not at all sure that Brian could keep up with these seasoned mountain climbers, all with an enviable body-mass index. They were keeping themselves in shape with regular climbs, whereas for Brian this had been a singular experience. This was yet another indication of Brian's strong determination and skill to master challenges that he set for himself.

Brian's use of our first names in his diary may seem odd. This actually got an early start in his life. When he first had difficulty pronouncing the word 'daddy' and other kids made fun of him for it, he simply referred to my name instead. No matter how he pronounced that, no one could find fault. Sue then got the same treatment.

Ordinarily parents would likely object to being called by their first names by their young children. Why did we not raise objections right away? Much later we found that this phenomenon was becoming commonplace in Germany among parents of the immediate post-war generation. This was explained as part of the anti-authoritarian thrust that was now taking hold there. Indeed I may well have been subject to those same sentiments. My anti-authoritarian bent was further spurred by my experience with my severe and rigid father. Never would my children be treated in the same way that I had been.

## MATHEMATICS AND ART

*I had my art class on Wednesday, and I was just reading the book for the class, titled* Drawing On the Right Side of the Brain *by Betty Edwards. She writes of teaching people to see like an artist does. She speaks of "left mode" and "right mode," utilizing the left and right brains respectively.*

*Mathematics is also like art, in that it utilizes the right brain. Lower levels of mathematics, like arithmetic, are done with the left brain. But, when one enters the world of higher mathematics, like trigonometry, and calculus, the need for the right brain becomes greater and greater. When a mathematician is solving a problem, very often he draws a picture for himself. This helps him find relationships between different parts of the problem, and it involves the use of one's spatial thinking ability, located in the right brain.*

*Spatial thinking is most important in art—not only in arts that work with three-dimensional objects (pottery, wood carving, sculpture), but also in arts like drawing, and painting. I have always done very well in arts that work on three-dimensional objects, but in drawing or painting I have always tried to think with my left brain. Three days ago, when I bought this art book, I came to the realization that this was not the right approach, and that the right brain is just as necessary here as in any other art.*

*Also, EEG biofeedback could help people in learning to use the right brain. My biofeedback training is mainly on my left brain, and it has helped me a lot in English class, and in thinking like left-brained people, which I don't do very well.*

Brian's journal [September 10,1987]

The prevailing mindset at the time was to train mainly the left hemisphere, proceeding on the basis of what was known and what had been tested in research. Sterman's work had established a beachhead on the motor strip in cortex, within one narrow spectral region of the EEG, and essentially everything else remained *terra incognita*. This caution was not entirely misplaced, as it subsequently took many years to map out the entire terrain. We did in fact make occasional tentative forays to the right motor strip, on the assumption that a well-behaved right hemisphere could help to tame an unruly left by virtue of network connections. Even though Brian found this rewarding, it was not systematically pursued.

Brian's journal is resumed with more consistency in the fall with his return to college. On September 22, we heard from Cal Lutheran that Brian had had a seizure in physics lab. So, we were apparently not done with seizures after all. This was a particular blow because it was a daytime seizure. The threshold for daytime seizures was higher for Brian. His seizures had been nocturnal. So this raised a concern that we weren't reliably on an upward track. We brought Brian home for medical evaluation. Then he returned to school.

## THE EDGE

*I have been on the edge sleep-wise. I kept myself on the edge of sleep deprivation even when I didn't have to for the purpose of school. My medication, since I am now taking 400mg, has kept me until today far away from the "edge"— seizure threshold. I was previously taking 300mg, and incremented it after a seizure that I had at 8:15 a.m. in the physics lab, no doubt from too little sleep. I have been on 400mg for the past four weeks. I only needed more than 400mg the night I had only 4 hours of sleep. When I have six hours of sleep I have no problems.*

*Today I had gone into the Health Service to get a check on my ears and throat, which have not felt good. I was told that I have a virus.*

*This evening I felt so tired around five o'clock, that I napped for three hours. I then watched the end of the movie* Fright Night, *and the movie* The House.

*I have been very close to the "edge" tonight, and was worried I would fall off it and into the ditch. Therefore I didn't talk all that much. It is a world where "mental powers" are small, but physical powers might be great. Thinking is not in full strength, but feeling and acting are at medium or full strength. Feeling is always at full strength. It is feeling that always triggered that foot to slip off the edge when I was young; now it is usually the onset of stress, mental stress, and lack of sleep.*

*Beneath this "edge" is a world where "thinking" is beyond reality, but acting remains within the sphere of reality. In the ditch, "thinking" is met with illusions and misconceptions. These illusions and misconceptions directly inhibit actions. Both "thinking" and "actions" are inhibited by "feeling," which is one of the major triggers of the psychotic mode.*

*Actions never leave the sphere of reality, but can be disabled. Thinking is always there, but can leave the world of reality. If actions are also disabled, then being in the ditch has no dangers, and the pleasant aspects of being in the ditch are the only things present.*

*If you stand above that edge, you are in a world of mental, emotional, and physical control. If you fall off the edge and hang there, you are in great danger, as your mental powers are small and your physical powers great. Climb down those crags in the ditch and make it to the bottom. You will be in a world where all three—emotional, thinking, and acting—will be of little strength and you can rest comfortably. But emphasize one and leave the others insignificant, and you will be met with disaster.*

Brian's journal [October 23, 1987 Friday night]

The combination of a poor sleep pattern, illness, and the trigger of horror movies once again steeps Brian into a maelstrom of instability that he struggles to describe. Is the core self, the watcher, intact during this maelstrom? The experience seems immersive, entirely consuming, hence the inherent danger for Brian.

## THE RIGHT BRAIN

*The right brain: it is the domain of the subconscious and the unconscious. I spent all day doing my art final; all hunger and other bodily needs disappeared while my right brain worked intensively at drawing. All your sense of alertness and sense of time disappear if you let yourself into the right brain mode. It is the same as dreaming in a way: Eight hours of intensive visualization or imagination of the objects I draw. Not one break to eat or go to the bathroom, or anything at all, except for a few words to some of the people who entered in the afternoon to do their art finals. But only very brief words did I have with anyone. Most people in the room were talking Norwegian.*

*Eight hours of intensive drawing is like the same time spent daydreaming. In the same way as waking up from a long sleep, you don't have much of an idea of how long you have been sleeping or intensively drawing. I missed a very important appointment with my employer all because of this intensive drawing or daydreaming.*

Brian's journal [Dec. 16, 1987 Wednesday night]

## SWITCHING SIDES

*Most people are in their left brain and are more alert and in a logical frame of mind. But the right is a more unconscious and imaginative side. Switching from one side to the other—from being left-handed to right-handed—is something few people ever try, and if they do, they do it when they are young. I am doing it in the middle of a semester of college.*

*This week I have devoted time to training my right hand, and eating and writing notes in class with my right hand. But being right-handed has bad as well as good sides to it. People who are right-brained tend not to be good students. The left brain, when stimulated to produce higher frequencies and perhaps also to be dominant, makes the transformation of ideas in the im- agination to English much easier, and possible when it might otherwise have been impossible. The mind is more analytical in nature when the left brain is dominant, more alert, and thinks fast- er. But although this is very nice, there also is a loss: you cannot have both sides working at full power. Therefore the right brain is not dominant when the left is. One's sense of who he is ap- pears to be in the right brain. When I am in my left brain for long periods of time, I have a feeling of losing my identity. Half of me is gone, half of my soul, my emotions. It seems like I might just stay left-handed.*

*Only one month ago, it felt as if I even lost some of my math abilities, so I think it is only a matter of learning to utilize both sides of the brain. When I was first breaking through, and be- coming dominant on the left side a month and a half ago, I felt a stimulation down my whole right side that felt sexual like that of climbing the pole in first grade.*

Brian's journal [2/26/1988, Friday night]

"One's sense of who he is appears to be in the right brain." This is huge. I recall a similar observation from Brian the first time Sue trained his right hemisphere, and now he observes this just from exercising his two hemispheres differentially. Writing with his right hand stirred up his left-hemisphere organization in new ways, and engaging with the visual arts stirred up the right.

When Brian first told us this, we didn't know where to go with it. Because the outside world was rather hostile to what we were doing in neurofeedback, we had hewed fairly closely to what past published research supported. Since the study of cognitive function involved the left hemisphere almost exclusively in those days, there was no road map for the right hemisphere. So it took us a long time to get around to working systematically with the right hemisphere.

Another thing that held us up was that the right hemisphere trained according to different rules. Until we figured that out, we did not train the right hemisphere optimally. In retrospect, Brian's most serious deficits needed to be addressed most of all with right-hemisphere training. But we did not have the necessary understanding during his lifetime.

Brian's observations on his own condition did help us move forward at various times. He was an excellent observer, and his brain was exquisitely sensitive to everything that we did. But prudence required that the first foray into new terrain always had a good justification.

## ROOMMATE TROUBLES

*For the past few months I have been living with Gary—since the beginning of December. He runs hurdles in track, is a business major, and calls himself "king of the assholes."*

*On the night of March fifth, I was convinced that this man is an asshole. He has been telling me again and again, "Do not close the door to the bathroom." He wants the bathroom to ventilate, which is fine with me. I often shut the bathroom door even though I do not care whether it is open or shut; it comes from habit. He told me three times last night not to shut the door, which means I must have shut it three times. The fourth time he found it shut he told me to open it, but I turned around and walked to my room ignoring him. As soon as I stepped back out of my room, he grabbed me by the Adam's apple, and tried to choke me, shoving me up in the corner of the wall. I was about to respond by fighting back, but he let go of me before I did that.*

*What had happened that night with Gary scared me. I thought he might try to harm me again. It even led me to be too excited because of the fear, and I had a nightmare that night that might have included an epileptic seizure. I woke up shivering in my blankets, and feeling a little weak for a few hours. I went to breakfast soon after I woke up, and I was shivering in there while I ate breakfast.*

*I told many other people, friends of mine, about what happened. Many of them referred to Gary as "that asshole" or "that jerk." Many of my friends suggested that I fight back, "Beat that wimp up," but that would just cause more trouble for me.*

Brian's journal [March 5, 1988]

Parents don't routinely get input on choice of roommates, but we also did not think this would be an issue at Cal Lutheran. Unsurprisingly, other families had made the same choice we did. We had placed a troubled adolescent in a benign environment, and other families had done the same. Here they had found each other.

Given the provocation above, Brian's restraint was laudable. Prior to neurofeedback, he would not have calculated the longer-term implications. Triggered by a brittle physiology, he would have reacted violently. Clearly, then, his violent propensities were a neurological phenomenon, not a function of the will or of his personality.

## THE GREAT CHAIN

*I am only a small part of a great chain, most of which I do not see. All around me I see trees, animals, rocks; I am a small part of this world. There must also be many other humans out there, so what is the possibility that I have value? None! I am insignificant. I do everything wrong while everyone else does everything right. Everyone is responsible for himself, but for no one else. I am responsible only for myself and as a result no one is responsible for me.*

*By the laws of nature we are all connected by this great chain. This is enough of a connection or interface with the world, so we as individuals are all disconnected. I am myself, and am not responsible for anybody else. No one loves me except for myself. That is why I am responsible for me, and I am not responsible for them.*

*It feels great to be sitting on the bottom and look up with smiles at the world in an effort to understand it, but knowing only that "you know nothing" and are on the bottom. You have no responsibility, for you are unimportant, and you are on the bottom. You never tell people what to do or try to change the world for you know that you know nothing, and don't have the right to do that. You accept the world for what it is, and continue to try to understand it and live by its laws. But you never go fixing it for you are nothing. You let things be as they are, and if you are not happy with the world, remember that that is your problem. "Everything is right." You must learn to adjust.*

Brian's journal [March 5, 1988]

Brian experienced wild swings in his mental state, and he recorded his thoughts even during his greatest moments of despondency in order to reflect on them later. It was all part of the effort to understand himself better. He surely did not expect these writings to be seen by others, at least not at this stage, so this material is as raw as it gets. Later he did agree that his story should be told, but of course he thought he would be in charge of telling the story.

## THE ART OF TRACKING

*This weekend at Nature Knowledge Workshop, my third, has been very concentrated in sense perception rather than knowledge; in feeling rather than seeing the wilderness; in hearing, touching, and smelling the wilderness. This weekend I got addicted to the "art of tracking." The most interesting part was doing the "fox walk" which was not only a style of walking but involved meditation as well.*

*In doing the "fox walk" one perceives the world with all his senses to the very best of his ability, as well as walking as quietly as possible. One looks straight forward using the blank vision to detect motion, listening to every sound, smelling every odor, delicately feeling the ground with the feet in every step. You walk on the outside of your feet concentrating your weight around the ball of the foot.*

Brian's journal [May 23, 1988, Monday]

## INCREASED PERCEPTION

*For over a year I have been able to feel whether my brain is producing the frequency that is reinforced on the EEG biofeedback instrument. My ability to sense it has been growing. Writing with my right hand has been my technique outside of the office for producing the frequency. About two weeks ago I tried a new technique that teaches me to produce it on both sides simultaneously rather than one, as writing does. I also train myself to do it all the time, day and night.*

*My technique involves an increased sense perception as practiced in tracking, certain martial arts, and by Indians. I was initially practicing this new awareness because I wanted to perfect my tracking skills. The technique is a whole new mind-set and involves not only listening to nature, smelling odors, seeing, and feeling the earth, but sensing the spatial position of everything, including every part of your body.*

Brian's journal [May 23, 1988]

The above was written at about the time when we delivered our first instrument to Margaret Ayers for testing. Brian was still training at Margaret's office. "Producing the frequency" is a reference to meeting the threshold for the size of the EEG signal within the training band of 15-18 Hz. Brian was very sensitive to the state of his brain, or shall we say, to the particulars of his dysfunction. He had come to know the correlation between how he felt and certain measures in the EEG.

The discovery of tracking was a watershed for Brian. Readers knowledgeable in the field of neurofeedback will recognize the similarity of this language to that used by Dr. Les Fehmi in describing "Open Focus"®. Open focus is an attentional skill that opens up our sensory receptive capacities, with implications for mental abilities, and even for mental health and for physical well-being. In the Open Focus exercise, the trainee deliberately broadens sensory awareness across all sensory modalities, including awareness of one's internal state. One consequence of entering this broadened state of awareness is a lowering of the level of arousal. The brain moves to a lower level of excitability.

The impact of these new perceptions on Brian is so strong that he recapitulates this new synthesis not twice, but three times in his journal:

> *Perceiving the world through the senses, feeling the earth in every step, smelling every odor, hearing every whisper, and visually perceiving all that can be seen in the scope of one's vision: this art has helped me sense and change my brain waves far beyond my own expectations, even reversing the dominance in my brain. Opening up the senses to the world is an awareness of oneself and the surrounding world, and is both mental and physical. It is primarily this awareness of oneself on the inside that has led to better brain performance. Practicing this awareness is far superior to other methods because of its applicability to whatever one is doing (awake*

*or asleep), and it will work on both sides of the brain simultaneously.*

### Brian's journal [July 10, 1988]

If practicing this awareness is far superior to other methods, in Brian's own experience, was it really necessary then for him to do neurofeedback? It is true that neurofeedback simply appeals to the natural processes of regulation within the brain that can also be trained in other ways. In principle one could just work with a variety of conventional brain training options. In practice, however, it is very much a question of where on the spectrum of mental competence we are working. The functioning brain may well be aided readily with techniques ranging from meditation practice and Open Focus to cognitive skills training.

As one moves down to lower levels of functionality, however, the case for neurofeedback strengthens. Les Fehmi, for example, typically teaches Open Focus with instrumental (neurofeedback) support. In Sweden, meanwhile, purely behavioral methods resulted in about 60% reduction in seizure incidence among children, which matches the gains reported in the literature for neurofeedback. From our vantage point, neurofeedback has the edge in terms of training efficiency, the gain per unit of effort expended. But ultimately it is not an either/or proposition, as Brian is finding.

It was the anti-convulsant medication that set the table for neurofeedback. And it was the neurofeedback that set the stage for Brian's multi-faceted agenda to improve his own brain function and brain stability. Neurofeedback was taking him to good places in terms of brain function, which he then wanted to consolidate by all available means. This he was pursuing through managing every aspect of his life, all of which was contingent on greater awareness of his own states of being. The neurofeedback had opened the door to what was possible on several levels, that of physiology and that of the mind and of the will.

## NEW FORM OF MEDITATION

*A new form of meditation has led to my breaking limits beyond my own expectations on the EEG biofeedback instruments. Writing had been my practice outside of the office, but it isolated frequency production on only one side of the brain. Now I have done some intensive work in training both sides of the brain simultaneously by practicing a new awareness of the world, a mindset related to that of tracking or in the martial art, Ninjitzu. Walking and sensing the world as an Indian or tracker would, I train my brain to produce the desired frequency on both sides all the time, day and night.*

*Sense perception of nature, smelling colors, feeling the earth, listening to every whisper and using all sight to understand the spatial position of everything—this has become a new way of seeing nature for me, and I am addicted.*

Brian's journal [July 10, 1988]

Here Brian talks about EEG biofeedback instruments (plural). In this time frame he is still getting sessions at Margaret's office, but he also has experience with our new instrument. By virtue of his awareness of brain wave activity, through his extensive EEG biofeedback training, Brian could make the connection with specific brain states, and in particular with brain wave activity that involves the whole brain. Uncannily, without the benefit of instrumentation Brian observed what Dr. Fehmi has been teaching for some years, namely that the state of "open focus" is associated with whole brain synchrony, a mode in which the entire cortex is driven more coherently, or in-phase, than would otherwise be the case. Dr. Fehmi demonstrated the connection by explicit training of brain-wave synchrony using multi-channel EEG biofeedback techniques, and showing that the brain-state so achieved was conducive to, and consistent with, "open focus." It could also be demonstrated that when a person achieved the state of open focus, the degree of brain-wave synchrony was increased over ambient values. Reference here is specifically to the famous alpha band, the dominant EEG frequency in the resting brain.

Brian's ability to connect his feelings and awareness of his own brain to specific brain wave activity was facilitated by our new instrument, which allowed him to observe his own EEG continuously while undergoing the training. It got to the point where Brian could tell us beforehand what his EEG would look like that day.

# 4

## CAL POLY
### JANUARY 1989-JUNE 9,1989

Brian took a semester off from school to attend the National Outdoor Leadership School
(NOLS) in Colorado. This was something he
had dearly wanted to do for some time. He had progressed in computer
science to the point where he needed advanced courses which were not
available at Cal Lutheran. He therefore transferred to Cal Poly in San
Luis Obispo. Since continuity was lost in any event, this seemed like
the right moment to fulfill his dream. Brian then started at Cal Poly the
second semester in January 1989.

The trip to the high country with NOLS was everything Brian
had hoped for. Unfortunately, he did suffer another seizure while on
a strenuous high-altitude excursion. After recovering for a day or so,
Brian resumed his participation. The journal continues with his return
to university.

## THE PHYSICAL CHALLENGE
### *Sleep Patterns*

*I am affected physically as well as mentally by messed-up sleep patterns. The parts of my body that I use the most in a coordinated manner are where my muscles twitch in a seizure. I use my hand a lot to write. My hand will have spasms and twitch when I go to sleep.*

*The way my sleep has been disturbed is that each night I go to bed around 10:30 p.m., and I am very tired after a long day. My roommate comes back at about 12:00 p.m. and he turns on the light. He may also have someone with him to whom he is talking. The light and any voices disturb my sleep. For a period of about an hour I am repeatedly awakened and fall back to sleep. I am never fully awake or asleep, and just at the right level of consciousness (arousal) to have a seizure. If I am really stressed out, my fingers and toes start twitching. My ankles and wrists may twitch.*

*Becoming left-brained and altering the way my brain functions through perceiving what it is doing is like subjecting myself to the habits of a child: lots of sleep, a feeling of innocence, and that I am discovering life. I am re-learning all the things I learned as a child: how to eat, go to the bathroom, brush my teeth, write. I am also aware of things that are normally involuntary: my breathing and controlling it, different thought processes, my brain's control of my immune system.*

*Having the ability to perceive how my brain is working, and constantly paying attention to it, burdens me. It is also necessary that I get good "concentrated" sleep, or I may not be able to take good readable notes in class. Whenever my effort towards maintaining good brain function slackens, my writing suffers. When I am done with classes for the day, and I relax and take a shopping trip at the bookstore, my signature is often not readable and only a squiggly line. If I had more concentrated brain function I would write my signature beautifully. My writing quality is directly related to how well my brain is working.*

*Changing the function of my brain I have found to be a very precarious undertaking. My body does all sorts of strange things if my brain does not maintain a concentrated, controlled mode of operation. If my dominance becomes at all shaky, I run into weird physical behavior and sensations.*

Brian's journal [January 10, 1989]

### States of Awareness During Seizures

*On the night of February 5, 1989, I had a seizure in which my left brain was doing very well, and my right brain was having a seizure. When I went to bed, my left brain was doing well, but my right brain was hurting a little with a slight headache. I decided to go ahead and sleep since my left side was well.*

*Shortly afterwards I slipped into a brief beginning of a seizure, and in a few seconds I was out of it. My left brain stopped the seizure promptly since it was doing so well and I felt strongly right-handed or left brain-dominant. Rather than being in a state of uncoordinated action and loss of motor control, I was actually doing well, and was very coordinated. I stood back up and tried to get back in bed. At first I walked around and I eventually made it back to bed.*

*My roommate got up quickly when I yelled "Oh no!" as I fell out of bed. He asked me if I was all right, and I responded, "Why do you keep on asking me that!" in an annoyed tone of voice. My roommate then asked me what I was doing, and*

*I wasn't sure, for I was in a sleepy, trance-like state. I think he asked me a second time, and I said whatever came to mind, probably what I was dreaming: "I'm looking for my underwear," as I walked about a little. Being annoyed by my roommate talking to me, I went to my bed to get away from him.*

*In the morning I awoke with a headache. I had no recollection of anything happening in the night. I noticed my sheets were all in knots, so I knew something happened. Maybe a seizure?*

*Later in the day my roommate asked me how I was feeling, and I said, "Fine. Why?"*

*He said, "You had a seizure last night."*

*Fred explained what happened, and it started to refresh some feelings I had of words and actions somewhere spoken in the last 12 hours. I remember today, very vaguely, some of the seizure.*

*From this experience I conclude that my brain is in one of two general states of awareness of the world when I have a seizure. One is a state of deeply perceiving and feeling the environment I am in. The second is a state of awareness of myself without much idea of what's going on around me.*

*The first state of awareness listed above has been the more common one in the past, but is worse than the second because of reduced motor control and ability to get myself out of the seizure. It is associated with seizures of both left and right brain, that is, seizures where both hemispheres are involved.*

*The second state of awareness, in which I am more aware of myself and of the present, I have more control. I usually get out of the seizure instantly, but can be left in a "sleepwalking" state of motor function. I have no concept of past or future, the world as I perceive it goes in and out of my mind with no recollection of past. I have almost no interpretation of my perceptions. From what my vision perceives I am aware only of the physical existence of the world but nothing beyond that. Other levels of interpretation that can be made at a subconscious state of awareness may occur. Interpretation of spoken words may occur, and I may respond to them.*

Brian's journal [January 10, 1989]

It may be startling to readers that Brian speaks so matter-of-factly of seizures. First of all, seizures are a fact of life for most people with epilepsy, whether or not they are on medication. Forty percent of those who are optimally medicated still have seizures. Secondly, the level of awareness Brian has throughout the seizures makes them less threatening to him than they may appear to outside observers. The seizures are always at night, with only a couple of exception over the past several years.

Moreover, they do not occur out of the blue. Brian is always aware when he is vulnerable to them.

One can argue that a higher level of medication might reduce the seizure incidence significantly. No one is better aware than Brian himself, however, of the cost/benefit ratio of such an increase in terms of his mental functioning. Not only was Brian unwilling to dull his brain to a greater extent, but he also felt it necessary to navigate the territory of his brain in order to learn what additional changes to make to increase his level of control. He would not be learning anything in a state of being zoned out by medication.

We as parents of course would have preferred less of a tight-rope act. When we made our feelings known, Brian would answer that he knew a lot more about his brain, and about the choices he was making, than we did. We simply were not in a position to insist. We had to agree that his approach was a cautious one. Brian was not a risk taker. Few undertake life with such a preoccupation with self-awareness and self-control as did Brian. We could hardly complain. In the final analysis, it did not matter what we may have wished. Brian was clearly making his own decisions at his age. One of the decisions he made was to keep us in the dark about most of the seizure-related events.

The claim by Brian that he could abort his seizure may also seem incredible. However, this is a common report by people with epilepsy. In Europe, systematic research is currently being conducted into behavioral strategies for preempting seizures. One of these studies was even sponsored by a Swiss drug company.

## THE SOCIAL DISCONNECT
### *Building Resistance*

> *Today was the last day of classes for spring quarter. Next week is finals.*

*The quarter has gone well. I expect to get A's in all my classes except speech. I am surprised that I stand at the top of two of my classes. The biofeedback that I practiced on my right brain during Easter break helped me build resistance to seizures. I have not had any more seizures this quarter, despite many attempts by my former roommate and current roommate to induce one. He would create such disturbances as poking me, slamming a pillow on my head, flipping the light on and off constantly for a minute or more; calling and letting the phone ring for a long time, and hanging up when I answer.*

*Every night sleep has been a deep, well-rested sleep. Many times when going to bed at midnight to get up at 8:30 a.m., I did not get to sleep until three hours later due to the many disturbances, and to my desire to listen in on conversations in the other room concerning my roommate's anger towards me. Although awake, the body is at rest, and it is much better than sitting up wide awake.*

Brian's journal [June 9, 1989]

Because Brian came to Cal Poly in the middle of the school year, he did not have much choice in roommates. Those who were left after all the socially-adept kids had paired up were living without roommates, and they probably needed to live alone. Either no one wanted to room with them, or they preferred their solitude.

We had been concerned from the start. When Brian moved into the room, the only evidence of any contact his roommate had with the English language was a Domino's Pizza menu. It did not look auspicious as an academic environment. We only heard about this harassment long after Brian had moved out.

*Last quarter started with seizures and changed into sleepwalking. This quarter has not seen any sleepwalking or seizure experiences.*

Brian's journal [June 9, 1989]

This history of ongoing seizure activity was largely unknown to us. We assumed that Brian would tell us about any such occurrences. It is quite likely that Brian interpreted the "sleepwalking" state as indicating progress in his mastery of the condition. He was probably unaware of the kindling model of seizure activity, in which every seizure contributes to making subsequent seizures more likely, so that they are progressively harder and harder to manage.

*My resistance to any seizures whatsoever this last quarter at Cal Poly, from April 3 to June 8, 1989, has been impressive. My roommate would allow people to stroll in and out of the room while I tried to sleep. When my prior roommate, Fred, would walk in, he attempted to startle me in hopes of provoking a seizure. Fred was never successful, but still believed I had seizures when he was not around. I was usually awake when he attempted to cause me to have a seizure, and this meant being awake until 4:00 a.m. Only when there was harassment past this time did I ever get awakened from sleep.*

*During the night from 11:00 p.m. until 4:00 a.m., I stayed conscious, kept my eyes shut, and kept myself relaxed. This ability to stay relaxed under all circumstances is what has allowed me to resist seizures when people are trying to cause me to have one. I am kept conscious by a subtle alertness to what is going on.*

*Often there were conversations that went on in the other room about my roommate's dislikes towards me. I would listen to the words of my roommate as he spoke about me. I would have liked to write down his words about me, but I could not do that if I wished to be getting rest. So this subtle alertness was basically an awareness of who was speaking and what was being spoken, also to who was present in the room or in the neighboring room. The words spoken were usually not remembered. They went into my mind and were comprehended, and then went out unremembered.*

Brian's journal [June 9, 1989]

A residue of all of Brian's prior difficulties was that he would be likely to hold himself responsible for any offense that he might give others. There was little sense of entitlement to be free from harassment by his roommate. Angry when she heard about what was going on, Sue told Brian in no uncertain terms: "Brian, you have a right not to be abused."

On later reflection, Sue realized that Brian's passivity in the face of such insults is something that might be expected of someone with an abuse history. And even though he had not been abused he might still have experienced his earlier life in that way. Brian indulged in a lot of self-blame, and there is little doubt that our early parenting, when his severe difficulties first surfaced, had put him in a real bind—imposing the burden to control his behavior when he was clearly unable to do so. Brian had been helpless in the face of our exhortations, and the fallout was the internalization of a thorough-going self-blame.

## *Making Contact*

> *Friday evening of that week, at dinner in the stalls, I attempted to make contact with someone at the same table. I caught his attention and held his interest. I spoke to him and soon we were having a nice conversation. I walked back with him to his room, where we talked about psychology and God and Christianity. Talking about Christianity, Jesus, God, and the words of the Bible took away my feelings of paranoia. I related my spiritual connection to nature to my connection to God. I related these two connections, and said they are both the same connection seen differently.*
>
> Brian's journal [June 9, 1989]

Just engaging with a stranger in conversation was worthy of commentary in Brian's journal. Something that comes so naturally to others is here a challenge of great import. No name is given, so it clearly did not lead to an ongoing connection. Literally nothing came easy to Brian—except possibly mathematics.

# BRIAN'S PHILOSOPHICAL MUSINGS
## Critical Thinking

*I am taking a class in critical thinking at Cal Poly. The definition in the book for thinking is "our active, purposeful, organized efforts to make sense of the world." From my experiences with different levels of conscious awareness, I do not agree that all thinking is purposeful organized efforts. As long as one has a conscious awareness of what is going on in the world around him, he is thinking. One level of consciousness may be close to sub-consciousness—day dreaming, for example—but it does not include sleep. In sleep, one's perceptions are a product of his own imagination, and he is not perceiving the world outside. As long as someone has a level of conscious awareness, whether fully conscious or partially conscious, he is thinking.*

Brian's journal [January 14, 1989]

Unsurprisingly, the book definition is the left brain's notion of thinking—purposeful and organized. What Brian realized perfectly well is that if the brain is at all in a position to think, it will do so. It can hardly do otherwise, as meditators know perfectly well.

## Both Sides of the Brain

*Everyone talks of people being either artistic or analytical. Music, drama, sculpture, painting, are examples of such artistic disciplines. Math, and all sciences based in mathematics, are analytical disciplines. Many associate the analytical with the left brain, and the artistic with the right brain, and believe that people are either one or the other, but not both. Although the artist and the analytical seem to be far apart, they are actually much closer.*

*Mathematics and music have been said to be related, and so are many of the other creative disciplines listed above. Many disciplines that are artistic are also analytical; those that are analytical are artistic too. Drawing becomes more analytical when it is directed towards representation of the physical world: that is, observing the three-dimensional world and copying it to a two-dimensional representation of it. In drawing the physical world, one must analyze it. The artistic side of drawing is the imaginative side of it. Physics involves much analysis, especially when used in disciplines that apply it, like engineering, but when one looks at physics aesthetically, and opens up his imagination, one sees an artistic side to it all.*

*Everyone has both an artistic side and an analytical side to their minds, although many seem to see only one side or the other.*

Brian's journal [June 9, 1989]

### The Spiritual and Physical Worlds

*How is the spiritual world related to the physical? Do the spiritual and physical worlds overlap or not? Man still does not understand how these two worlds are connected, or even if they are. Because we do not really know, it is best to consider them separate. When man understands scientifically what gives a person with a body and brain consciousness, then we will be on our way to understanding this connection. In the spiritual world there is communication on a subconscious level between different consciousnesses.*

Brian's journal [June 9, 1989]

The matter-of-factness with which Brian treats communication between different consciousnesses is refreshing. Sometimes it just takes a fresh eye to see the obvious, to go where an older generation fears to tread.

## THE WRONG TRIBE

Brian returned home for the summer to work on software for the new system, which we decided to call NeuroCybernetics.

### The Family Business

*I am home this summer because my family wants me to work in the family business. I have been a little reluctant to do it for several reasons: no pay, no experience of going through a job interview, and getting a real job. I have consented to do it only because I do believe in the success of this business, and I do feel like I should be a part of it. I also feel too much at home. Next year, to do something different, I should get a job elsewhere, like at San Luis Obispo. I will feel better there. Currently I feel sick of being dependent on my parents.*

Brian's journal [July 4, 1989]

"Brian, if you could only know how much difference your work has meant to so many people around the world."

How one wishes to have that one more conversation.

Brian was working on software for the Amiga to bring video feedback into the picture, and to displace the green and red lights we had started with. The Amiga was much more suitable for video processing than the PC. This effort was crucial for us to move forward, and it was a good match to Brian's own career objectives in computer science.

From our perspective, he was also very proud of what he was accomplishing. Among other things, he was working with a superb software writer in Edward Dillingham. Software is a young man's game, by and large, and here we had one of the few white-haired guys still keeping up with the young tigers.

One reason for Brian's concern may well have been the realization that we were in fact rather dependent on his success in the software task. By this time we had our first clinical operation in Encino, but the income from that was hardly sufficient to sustain us. I had just given up my job in aerospace earlier in the year in order to devote full time to this project, so we were up against the cold reality that the instrument needed to succeed rather quickly.

> *The time is coming for me to leave home. Every day I sense that my father treats me like I can no longer be changed, taught, and whatever idio-syncrasies I have are here to stay. I feel like I do not belong at home, like I have been misplaced. I am with the wrong tribe.*
>
> Brian's journal [July 3, 1989]

It is painful to confront Brian's judgment on our relationship even across the span of so many years. A parent in our situation cannot help but rake over the past with a view toward what could have been done differently. Fortunately memory is kind. Much is simply beyond recall, and what is recalled can be progressively reframed. Not in this case. This was a case of Brian misreading my intentions, but in any event this was his reality at the time, and I was not aware of that. Before he went off to college our relationship had indeed become more transactional in nature. We were having sober discussions about the issues, and the issues were often weighty. These discussions probably lacked warmth, to be sure, so that the mere expression of concern on my part could be read as disapproval.

As it happens, in my own life I was also certain that I could never please my father. Only years after his death did I find out that he had shown a "proud-father" side to his colleagues at work and at church. I certainly never got to see it. This experience made me determined to do things differently with my own children. And yet here I was, apparently mirroring my own father's behavior. Mere awareness of the issue is not enough to bring about escape from one's upbringing. Here I even lacked awareness of how my own manner was being interpreted.

*I am sick of home, and sick of being in front of the computer. I need to get outside of this isolated cave with an Amiga computer. I need to get out to the city where I can meet people, women, and have a good time. Developing my communication skills is very important, and I need to start doing that now.*

*This afternoon that I spent at the park and the pier in Santa Barbara was a reminder to me that I need to get away from the isolation of my room. Subconsciously both my parents and I are aware that I do not fit in with them anymore. I need to go meet other people my age, fix up that bike and go explore L.A. People have a need to socialize, and I have spent too many years isolated from the social atmosphere.*

*Besides the fundamental need for others in your life, I do not fit with my parents because they condemn the goal of mine, to develop my communication skills, and the study of other languages. Their reason, I believe, is my poor grades in past years in subjects related to this endeavor. But if I have already made remarkable changes with the EEG Biofeedback, I do not see why further success is not possible. I believe in my ability to succeed, despite my parents' doubts, and I will continue to pursue my educational goals, perhaps without my parents.*
Brian's journal [evening, July 4, 1989, 6:40pm]

I recall one episode in particular from this time. Brian and Ed Dillingham are sitting in our large living room, each at their own computer, Ed at his PC and Brian at his Amiga. The communication link is not working. Ed suspects Brian's code must be the problem, he being the novice here.

"I am confident of my code. I have checked it over and verified it," Brian insisted calmly but firmly. The problem, in fact, was elsewhere. Remarkable also was the lack of defensiveness and anger at being challenged in this way by his mentor. The fulminations were all coming from Ed. Brian had truly made progress. And his code had indeed been working perfectly.

*Last night, driving home, my father asked me if my driving permit was still good, and said I should practice if it is still good. So the picture does not look as bad as it seemed yesterday.*

Brian's journal [July 6, 1989]

Brian and I would drive down to the Sepulveda flood control basin in order for him to practice driving. We picked a remote area, and noticed quickly that we were being ogled from various quarters. Now it is true that we were driving an interesting car, an old 1969 BMW 2800, but this is Los Angeles, where it takes an exotic car indeed to turn heads. We had probably driven right into the middle of a bunch of drug dealers, and they had to be concerned that we might be there to monitor their activities. After all, Brian looked too old to be learning how to drive. So we were probably disrupting the flow of business the whole time we were there. But still we came back again and again. It was a nice place to practice driving.

Here we appear to be on an uptick on Brian's emotional roller coaster. This may have something to do with the nearness to the goal in the software development. Or it could have to do with the driving practice, which immediately changed the tone of our relationship. We had had so few opportunities of that kind in the past.

Most commonly the father-son bond forms around sports. But the T-ball had gone badly, and an attempt at youth soccer had been a disaster. Brian never developed a sense of the flow of the game and where he fit into it. The coach was exasperated with him, and the only remedy was to flee the premises, never to return. Our togetherness was usually out in the natural environment, but these were always more communal ventures rather than father-son activities.

One such opportunity did arise. We were visiting Wheeler Peak in the Great Basin National Park in Nevada, and both Brian and I were ready for more when Sue was fatiguing in the hike toward the peak. The two of us found ourselves boulder-hopping over a field that seemed to stretch endlessly before us as we approached the amphitheater of rock faces that is Wheeler Peak. When we finally turned back, the gently downward sloping expanse of boulders beckoned. We started running, leaping from boulder to boulder. We egged each other on to run even faster. It was impossible to gauge more than the very next footfall and perhaps the one after that. Our competitiveness was unspoken. If one of us ran faster, the other moved to catch up. And thus we flew down the slope at flat-out running speed. It was madness; but it was also bliss.

My biggest surprise upon first reading the journal was seeing the importance Brian placed on the father-son relationship. Those special moments like the one on Wheeler Peak were probably too rare.

## Failure

*With my experience of failure, and of having no friends, my English skills never really developed, especially with respect to speaking. My beliefs led me to be a failure in many circumstances. Some of these failures were detrimental to me. Others were of no consequence.*

*Unfortunately this belief led to another fail-
ure this summer which was detrimental: hitting
my head. All because of this idea that I "have to
do" something. I get angry about "having to do"
something, when I was only asked.*

*Being at home often strengthens this belief. I
feel that I should not live at home. In the future
I hope to have an income, and live elsewhere.
I felt like staying away from home before coming home this summer, and during the first few
weeks at home. But most of this summer at
home has been very interesting and fun.*

Brian's journal [September 12, 1989]

Brian's life was a roller-coaster of highs and lows. The lows were at times despairingly low. One also sees the concreteness with which he surveys his options. One has the sense that many of the things that become second nature to us as we mature were still entries in a rulebook for him. When life did not make sense, sense had to be imposed.

The anger that Brian speaks of surfaced from time to time, but we did not experience it as being directed at us or at me specifically. The anger could equally well be self-directed, resulting in self-punishment. The message Brian got from his life in the household was that expressions of anger were not okay. To illustrate, there had been one time when Sue and I raised our voices to each other in mock anger, and Brian was so perplexed by this that he hastened to inquire whether we were thinking of getting divorced! There had been no precedent for this in his experience. As for the yearning for independence from home and family, that is surely a positive sign in someone who has already spent a couple of years in college.

In a person with a vulnerable brain, any kind of head injury is of concern. By now we know that even heading the ball in soccer can have deleterious consequences for the vulnerable brain, and that a concatenation of many such headers can even create such a vulnerability. Normally brain function recovers substantially from such insults over time, but deficits do accumulate in the brain at risk. In this event, the concern about the minor head injury quickly subsided, rightly or wrongly.

### The Mazes Game (Pac-Man)

*Finishing Pac-Man up this summer before going back to school has been the most stressful part of my summer. The last five days have been "push, push, push" to complete Pac-Man as quickly as possible.*

*I was feeling overstressed by all this. I ended up having a seizure. Whether or not this seizure resulted from the stress, I would still call it "HELL." Everyone else is complimenting me, and my family wishes to celebrate. I feel like I am glad to be done with the torture chambers and would rather not think about it. I hope these heartless people will not put me through such "hell" again.*

Brian's journal [September 13, 1989]

The then-popular Pac-Man game inspired our first computerized feedback video game. In order to distinguish our design from the well-known standard, we referred to ours as Mazes. Among ourselves, we often fell back on the familiar terminology, even though our Mazes game actually bore little resemblance to Pac-Man.

Sue and Kurt had jointly designed a set of ten or so different mazes, through which the Pac-Man-like blob would move, scarfing up dots along the way. Its speed and its brightness were controlled by the EEG training variable. Whenever the EEG became unruly and stepped beyond certain bounds, the dot-munching fish-mouth would stop entirely and go dark.

Kids were delighted to be in a position to make a video game go directly with their brains. And whenever the blob stopped, they would be motivated to get it going again. We took advantage of kids' natural tendency toward competitiveness, and their natural preference for movement over stasis. Adults reacted much the same way.

# 5

## CAL POLY

*Today we went to a fancy Chinese restaurant in Santa Barbara with Art Cota and Lois Boylen. One of the five trays was a seafood plat-ter, and in the seafood platter there were some red peppers. I ate a little of one of the red peppers. My father then said, "He has too much confidence and too little sense." My mouth was soon burning hot and my eyes watered. I wanted to see how hot a red pepper feels when eaten straight. My confidence is certainly not too high, and my sense, well sometimes it may not be what it should be due to beliefs of "failure." Too much confidence is something I have en-countered only a few times in life, but too little confidence is something I encounter every day.*

Brian's journal [July 3, 1989]

Lois Boylen was a brilliant hematologist who struggled with lupus, and was also susceptible to seizures. We had met through the Natural Science Section of the Sierra Club, where she had served as a naturalist. The plasmaphoresis she had to undergo regularly to purge her system of excess antibodies also depleted the blood of Tegretol, so after every episode of plasmaphoresis she would come for neurofeedback to buffer herself against seizures. Just before she succumbed to the lupus years later, she told us that she was saddened not to be around for the further development of our field. Her husband Art was the first person we ever worked with successfully in the treatment of sleep apnea.

## COMING TO TERMS WITH THE INNER WORLD
### *Life Goal*

*Unity with the world; being at one with the world; loving life because of the enjoyment of the experience; neither good nor bad, the experience is wonderful because it furthers my understanding of the world. My needs extend no further than my basic physical needs for water, air, food, and love. There is no right, or wrong; good or bad; life just is. I am the source of all my joy. Whatever the world thinks of me does not matter or affect my joy. I love nature, and nature loves me. I do not stand above everyone as superior, nor do I stand below as inferior; I just am.*

*Being at unity with the world, I can be whatever I wish. The world is plentiful, and all can be whatever they wish; the only requirement is your desire and motivation.*

*My life goal as I saw at an early age was to learn and understand how nature works, and to teach that to others. By nature I mean all sciences underlying how it works. I, of course, do not expect to fully understand nature, nor do I claim to be right. I am always open to others' ideas, and there is always more to learn.*

*What I have said thus far, explains my beliefs and goals in my early years up to age seven. But at that time my younger sister died. I could not understand why so many children teased me. My enlightened childhood was over. For more than a decade of time I lived miserably, and angry mostly towards myself because I realized that something had totally changed. My hate grew, and I contemplated suicide, although I never decided to attempt suicide. Some of my beliefs that I had held while young I continued to hold. My love in certain respects was still there.*

*Now, 13 years later, I am becoming enlightened once again. But it is slow and I am not completely there yet.*

Brian's journal [July 6, 1989]

I am curious as to the intended meaning of the word enlightened here. Since he associates it with his early childhood it cannot refer to a state of knowing. Rather, it likely refers to a state of innocence, of natural equilibrium with his environment, of holism. The child growing up in a secure ambiance takes this for granted. It is the natural state. The state of balance with nature, of fitting in appropriately, must later be reacquired by Brian as a deliberate intention.

### Twitching and Cracking

*Every area of my body experiences cracking of joints, and when under tension, twitching of muscles. To prevent both twitching and cracking one must have an awareness of his body. I have noticed that to have control of a particular muscle, I must have control of its opposite. To prevent cracking of joints, I must be aware of several muscles surrounding that joint.*

*Muscles twitch when they are expanding from a contracted position, but not being stretched. If my leg is fully extended, my quadriceps on the leg is fully contracted, and as I bend it back to a 90 degree angle at the knee it may twitch if I am not sufficiently aware of my hamstrings. By activating the hamstrings through an awareness of them, I cause the opposite muscle, quadriceps, to relax.*

*My chest or abdominal muscles may twitch when reclining from sit-ups during exercises. This can be prevented by being more aware of muscles in the lower, middle back, causing abdominal muscles and chest muscles to relax.*

*To prevent joint cracking, I must be aware of several different muscle pairs. It is generally a subset of all muscles surrounding the jointdepending on the direction of movement.*

Brian's journal [July 29, 1989]


## A French Dream

*My sleep is becoming more relaxed every day, and my dreams are becoming ever more vivid. Last night I dreamed I was living as a guest in a French household in France. The house was a three-story mansion, and the owner was a lawyer. There were several women prostitutes in the house. The house appeared to me to be more like an apartment with many public facilities (public only to those that have a room in the mansion). There were several Jacuzzis in the mansion; each was unique with its own spiritual feeling surrounding it. The mansion was full of idols, giving it spiritual diversity. Although the house remained structurally the same, with few exceptions, going up and down the staircase, the shamans, gurus, and other spiritual leaders would be totally different each time I arrived on the third floor.*

*The three floors of the mansion each were very different. The top floor was the spiritual world with shamans, gurus, and other spiritual leaders. The second floor was "love and passion"; all leisure activities were on this floor. On the bottom floor were the serious and scientifically minded people.*

*I was almost always on the second and third floors. I would alternate back and forth between them; going to the other when the one had become boring. Only when a prostitute woman, to whom I was attracted and was having a conversation with, went to the first floor did I follow and arrive on the first floor.*

Brian's journal [July 29, 1989]


## Beliefs and Values

*Who am I? What are my beliefs and values? My life is an on-going restructuring of beliefs, values, and sleeping patterns. Sleeping patterns were the first screwed up thing to cause me to have epilepsy. Restructuring of beliefs and values is a result of a change of brain dominance: my left brain is now the dominant side of my brain. My personality may change any time. It changes every time I have a seizure. I want to throw away the set of values I have now, and get a better one; the real one that was originally me.*

*Most people's brains are more stable and don't come out with different personalities from day to day.*

*Over the years of childhood I have developed only bad beliefs and values. The only values to keep are the ones that are innate. My parents have only caused me to have bad beliefs. I must clear my mind of all these beliefs and values that have accumulated and start with my original and good beliefs. The experience is all there to quickly build the next set. But it will not be too quick. The real barrier is not developing the new beliefs, but discarding the old ones.*

*When I was only six years old my mind was free of all this stuff that clutters my brain and dominates my life. It is my intention to free my mind of this stuff. The biggest factor to this whole glob of stuff cluttering my brain and beliefs is the belief that people are angry at me, and wish to hurt me. This belief is simply an assumption that "when people look at me they must be annoyed or angry since there is no way they could be glad to see me." This belief (developed at age eight), and other beliefs acquired later, I intend to empty my mind of them.*

Brian's journal [August 31, 1989]

This puts a different light on Brian's feeling that I was always looking at him with an angry expression. But often I was angry, or at least exasperated. And those events would be the most sharply remembered.

### Head Injury

> The effect of hitting my head at Raging Waters has been interesting but unpleasant. My EEG still has a lot of the beta frequency it had before, but there is also a lot of delta frequency present (very low frequency, 1-3 Hz). The delta peak is enormous, and stands 20 times higher (at least) than the next highest peak in the low alpha region. On other days the delta seems to be the only thing In my brain. My left brain is currently dominated by delta, but my right is dominated by alpha.
>
> Brian's journal [August 31, 1989]

Excessively large EEG signals at low frequencies are indeed features of brain injury. Brian was still at home at this time, and was able to track it. Typically there will be some recovery over a period of weeks and months, even without the help of neurofeedback. With neurofeedback, matters proceed more quickly, and likely progress to a more complete recovery of function.

### Teaching Philosophy

> The teaching philosophy of Cal Poly is "Learn by Doing." In view of this philosophy, I chose to come here. Terry also chose to go to Cal Poly because of this philosophy. But, Learn WHAT

*by doing? I do not want to be a robot because of doing computers all the time. A balance of computer science and humanities is necessary. A balance between specific and general. A balance between liberal and specialized. Is one getting a real education here at Cal Poly in the Engineering majors?*

*According to an editor of Mustang Daily, there are two types of educations at Cal Poly, real education, and pseudo education. The editor says that as a student, you will hear the "Learn By Doing" philosophy so much that you will be sick of it.*

*I often feel that Cal Poly may be somewhat too specialized in Engineering majors. But I will continue because I want the academic challenge that only specialized schools offer. I miss the liberal philosophy of Cal Lutheran.*

Brian's journal [September 16, 1989]


## Back to School

*Yesterday I arrived back at Cal Poly, and brought my books and met one of my roommates, Dan. Today I slept in late getting a lot of rest. Later, Dan and I went shopping, and had something to eat at McDonald's.*

*My new roommates look very friendly and I believe this year will go better than last year. I am glad to be off campus. I think I will never live on campus again.*

*Dan is a biology major. He is Oriental and enjoys cooking his own food. His mother insisted he eat with chopsticks. I offered to eat with chopsticks some rice that he cooked yesterday. I eventually got tired of using chopsticks.*

*Terry is a chemistry major. Terry just arrived around mid-afternoon today. I expect to get along well with him. He needs a lot of sleep like I do. Terry is a serious student, I've heard.*

*With friendly roommates and a good environment to sleep in, I feel that this year will be a good one, better than last year.*

Brian's journal [September 16, 1989]

### Volatile Brains

*My brains are volatile. Think certain thoughts now, and a few months later my beliefs might be tweaked so that I have a new personality. Most people do not have such volatile brains that their personality changes from day to day.*

Brian's journal [September 17, 1989]

Brains plural? Personality changes? We know that we contain multitudes. Brian is seeing a subset of these many selves as semi-autonomous entities, as something distinct from the core self. The very fact of their volatility serves to give hope that positive change is possible.

## Self-Realization

*Yesterday I had a self-realization experience. I am beginning to see God. I am now certain that I no longer need my medication. For so many years I have wondered if I would ever be able to get off this medication. I am now certain that I will, without doubt.*

*"Kriya Yoga" calms the mind and makes it possible for one to reach a "COSMIC CONSCIOUSNESS" in one's lifetime. There exists in this practice a cleansing of one's soul and mind, and redirection of the life force. Mastery of breath is one of the keys to this practice, and probably the most important key. For spiritual, physical, and mental well-being I wish to study Yoga and practice Yoga in the future. Meanwhile, until I do, I will practice my own form of meditation.*

*The "Cosmic Force," or Creator, or Mother Nature, what is this creator?*

*Is there really God? For so long I have felt spiritually a part of every living organism I could see; that there existed communication between me and the plant, or animal. This communication with nature was the beginning of my communication with God. Although I disagree with many other people's ideas of what God is, and how he created the earth and life. I have wondered if this communication between me and nature was God as others know God. Yes, I believe it is the same God even though many others have such different ideas of what God is.*

*Whether I will appear any different in personality or behavior as a result of the changes I am undergoing, I am not sure. But it is certain that changes are occurring, and I notice them as remarkable changes to my life.*

*The last two nights were experiences in blessed sleep. I have slept as deeply and divinely as ever. Two nights ago I dropped my Tegretol dosage from 500mg to 400mg. Because of the risk I face anytime I decided to decrease my dosage, I took extra precautions by meditating and praying. I prayed to God as I lay in bed before sleep. I was deeply relaxed; nothing would have awakened me from my deep sleep. The following night I had another similar experience. On the night of October 21, I was going to sleep with an incredibly strong feeling of invitation to have a deep blessed sleep. I began to feel like the "single eye" was materializing in my eye brows.*

Brian's journal [October 22, 1989]

### The Dark Side

*Through my experiences I have seen the "dark side," possession by the Devil. Everyone disbelieves you even if you always tell the truth. Everything fails because of the wrath, frustration and lack of esteem. My spiritual path in life has gone through the depths of the devil's possession, and will now glide up to the world of good. I have seen the world of disbelief and distrust in myself, and thus in others' attitudes towards me. Somewhere ahead lies the beginning of a life of trust; trust in myself, in others, and in others' trust towards me.*

Brian's journal [October 25, 1989]

Possession by the Devil. This is the Biblical description of seizures, no doubt formulated by outside observers. But the sense of being possessed by a foreign entity was apparently also part of Brian's inner experience of these events. Throughout his course of development Brian is rescued time and again by the realization that he is not reducible to his behavior. He is not to be identified with the "personality" that is apparent for others to encounter. His destructive behaviors are not implementing his intentions. It was he himself who needed to recognize this dual reality in first instance, because this is what kept him alive early on.

There is the self- versus non-self dichotomy here, and there is the good versus evil dichotomy. The challenge is to allow the "good" self to emerge while containing as best one can the "evil" non-self. In real life, the division is not always so apparent. The split-brain studies of Roger Sperry and Michael Gazzaniga and others have shown how the left hemisphere confabulates to make sense out of experience, even if it has only limited information. Thus, if the right hemisphere is amused by what only it has been allowed to witness, the left brain will still concoct a story to make that response seem appropriate in the frame of whatever information it has available.

By the same token, when Brian's right-hemisphere emotional circuitry erupts into "evil" undertakings, the left hemisphere will rush to rationalize what is being done. "He looked at me funny, so I hit him." Even as the left hemisphere knows and accepts the rules ("always tell the truth"), the left hemisphere can also be drawn into conspiracy with the right. The self and the non-self are ineluctably coupled. Hence Brian's dilemmas. His emerging self lacks a secure foundation. It is as if his brain is living through a perpetual earthquake.

### Vision Quest

*People of my time do not seek vision quests. Shamans in Indian tribes do; gurus in the Far East do; but not Americans. People are mostly tied up with the television establishing their goals for them. But this is not so for me.*

*A vision quest became crucial, as the only answer to the problems I have faced during my childhood: Having epilepsy; being possessed by the devil; appearing to be mischievous. Searching for an answer was essential. No one else could realize or understand my problem. People thought I was a naughty child trying to deceive them. Only I could realize that something more subtle had caused me to do things without intending to do them. My angry emotions on the surface of my "self" were all people saw, but deeper within the "self" I was still loving people and life. I lost all my friends, and the only answer was for me to find the "way" through my own search.*

*I often isolated myself in the woods to think. I would sit for hours at a time, alone, searching for answers. I searched for an answer to where I was headed in life. Death? Suicide? Electric chair? Nomad? Mental institution? Was I destined to die soon? Perhaps people will mistake me for a criminal. Maybe my parents would send me to a mental institution for mentally ill people. Lastly, perhaps I would escape this labyrinth of trouble by leaving and becoming a nomad.*

*Answers to questions posed were reached by one of two means: (1) Strictly logical, through reason; (2) Through the depths of the heart, seeking answers from "mother earth," through meditation. Answers were never obtained through emotional means. All answers from the heart were also considered by the reason before being used.*

*Time spent alone in search of better understanding of the "self" is valuable. I can no longer feel that I am complete and really "me" without time to understand my "self." By deeply knowing the "self" one appreciates life under all*

*circumstances. Material things become insig-*
*nificant. For deep down only the "self" really*
*matters.*

Brian's journal [October 30, 1989]

"Deep down only the self matters." And the essence of self is surely our emotional core more so than the intellect. Yet Brian's emotional being is being buffeted by his unstable physiology to the point that his understanding of himself continually migrates. It can never settle down.

### *Mental Confusion at School*

*What am I getting out of school? Not what I should! I am getting a sufficient education in terms of what is expected by others. But I am not learning what I am potentially able to digest into my repertoire. I am not blaming the school but myself. Cal Poly is challenging, and there is nothing to complain about on the part of the school. But I am on anti-convulsant drugs for epilepsy. The drug I take makes me drowsy, confused, and depressed.*

*My depression causes me to question the teacher's words. In almost all my classes I frown and turn away from what the teacher says looking at me. My expression says to the teacher that I am angry and displeased. When I ask a question, I quickly interrupt the teacher when he/she answers.*

*Often words go through me and I am con-
fused. I have spells of mental confusion. Thus I
do not digest as much from a lecture as I should.
Drowsiness causes me to drift off from lectures.
This is usually a product of the emotional depression which initiates the loss of attention. Realizing that I am not learning what I am potentially
capable of, I should focus on solving the medical problem so that I can operate at full potential. I should eliminate this depression so I can
be more.*

Brian's journal [October 31, 1989]

What an incredible sense of self-awareness Brian was developing here. There was a lot of variability in brain function from moment to moment that was all below the threshold of seizures, and Brian was doing his best to encompass it all, operating at once at the level of engagement with the incoming information, and at the same time trying to maneuver his brain into a receptive state. This is a difficult thing to pull off, because at the level of consciousness we don't timeshare all that well.

### A Nomad

*Where will I go in life? Have I committed myself
to a spiritual, nomadic life? A life in which I seek
wisdom, knowledge? My life will definitely ad-
here somewhat to a path of seeking knowledge.
But to a spiritual path? Is this financially and ethi-
cally possible? Or will I commit myself to a wife
and children?*

*Since my life has been burdened with epilepsy and medication; implying depression, anger, isolation, and absolute distress; I shall continue to seek what I have sought through much of my childhood. Time alone in the woods to think and meditate is what I seek: To reflect on life. I have become so attached to the spiritual world, that I do not want to leave it. I wish to find the connection between the spiritual and the physical worlds.*

*Sometime in my life I may start to think more about family. But I think this is still far away.*

Brian's journal [November 3, 1989]

### Happiness in Moderation

*Being happy and content with life is good, but happiness must not be taken too far. Happiness is good when it is mild, but if one is carried away by happiness his awareness is cut off. Happiness in the extreme (bliss) is emotional and sensual perfusion of the mind. During bliss one's mind is permeated by specific awareness, thought, and sensation. Thus one is ignorant of all else while in bliss.*

*Bliss appears in different forms. One form is different from another because it consists of different awareness, thought, and emotion. A Yogi-Christ experiences bliss while meditating on*

*God. An American might experience bliss while taking drugs. One may experience bliss naturally when being carried away with some form of happiness. If one experiences bliss while undergoing an acute experience of awareness, thought, and sensation then bliss is acceptable. But bliss is so intense in its ability to separate one from his environment that bliss for its own sake should be avoided. Any kind of bliss can be taken too far. Bliss should be an infrequent experience. Do not spend too much time in bliss.*

Brian's journal [November 9, 1989]

A recurring theme is that Brian feels the need to moderate all emotional excursions—both high and low—in order to manage. His need is so dire that sometimes he wants to suppress emotional responding altogether. What has become clear to him over time is that strong emotional responses are capable all by themselves of triggering his excursions into instability. It does not matter so much whether these excursions are in a positive or negative direction.

### *Temporary Life Goal*

*Today was Thanksgiving, but as usual I have spent much of my "thinking energy" thinking about my epilepsy and where I am headed in life. This evening I have tried to explain to my parents and uncle Hans where I really am headed, what kind of changes have been occurring, what kind of changes will occur, how who I really am is different from who I appear to* be, and why the continuation of this pursuit of change is important to me.

Where I am headed in life is my biggest question, since I often wonder whether my life is worth it. But at age two I had a vision of my goal in life. That vision however left me. My question about life is in regard to meeting the expectations set up after having the vision. I must do everything I can to meet those expectations, and thus fulfill my vision, to the extent that I understand it. If I can determine in any way that meeting up to this vision is impossible then death is justified. But this cannot be determined, so life is just, and suicide is unjust. Life and death are not topics I usually talk about, but the topic demonstrates my commitment to my vision.

I ran into an obstacle in my life path, and it interfered with my commitments. This brought about the question of how to revise my goals to meet the vision's expectations. Basically, I had to eliminate whatever had possessed me (epilepsy). I was certain that it was possible. I am still certain of it today. So I have a "temporary life goal" in which I am trying to eliminate epilepsy. This goal is temporary because I will only stick to it as long as epilepsy stands in the way of meeting the expectations set forth by the

*vision. Once the obstacle is out of the way I will
continue on my appropriate life goal.*
Brian's journal [November 23, 1989]

### Religion

*Today I have been reading* The Religions of Man
*by Huston Smith. Reading about Hinduism, the
Hindu religion has four classifications for the
wants of men. These are pleasure, success,
duty to society, knowledge of the infinite.*

*The first of these, pleasure, seems to be
one of the big motivators of people these days.
Pleasure seekers, and sensation seekers, both
are in this first classification. With how many
people are into sex and drugs these days, pleasure seekers constitute a large part of our culture.*

*Success, victory, or power constitutes the
second classification. This is the second large
motivator of today; together with the first these
two classes are "The Path of Desire."*

*I feel separated from the path of desire. Pleas-
ure and success are not what I seek. I am inferior, and I expect to work hard to make a living.
Life is not an easy trip. To make life rewarding
I must stick to values, commitments, and work
hard; enjoying myself while at work.*

*The third and primarily the fourth classifica-*
*tions represent me. I am a knowledge seeker,*
*but I wish, on the side, to do one duty for society:*
*teach. The only kind of greatness I seek is that of*
*discovery in the sciences. I wish to have children*
*in my life, but sex should not be practiced for any*
*other purpose than having children.*

*While I seek knowledge, I also seek to be*
*physically active in my life. Being physically fit is*
*as important as education of the mind.*

Brian's journal [December 9, 1989]

We did not give Brian a religious upbringing. Sue was put off early on by the categorical rejection of evolution by her Junior High School classmates in St. Louis. I, on the other hand, had been brought up in the most conservative of Lutheran denominations, the Missouri Synod. I experienced the value of the community that had been created in our church. That community had warmly welcomed us when my mother and I first came to this country, just as it had welcomed my father previously. It was important in our lives for many years. And yet faith in a personal God became ever more difficult for me over time. Finally all vestiges of such a faith drained out when I held Karen's dying body. This suffering did not make sense in any universe guided by an omnipotent and benevolent being. We were in the grip of events subject to impersonal forces. And yet I remain persuaded that we live in a universe with a spiritual dimension. The materialist assumption of science is an operational necessity, not a demonstrable fact.

Even in the absence of any kind of institutional framework and support for our value system, it appears that Brian broadly shares the values with which Sue and I have lived our lives.

## Thinking

*At school I spent much of my time thinking, and my roommates agreed that I thought too much. Perhaps it wasn't too much absorption in thought, but I did reduce my awareness of the outside world too much. Often I was not aware of what was happening around me because of too much inner-directedness. I focused too much on what my brain was doing, how I felt, what I thought, and what I believed. I was often unaware of where I was walking, whether other people were walking by, and I took a long time to respond to people saying hello. There is so much to be aware of, one must choose what he wishes to focus his awareness and perception on. I am trying to become aware again of what I often have been unaware of.*

*While sometimes I think really intensely, at other times I open up my field of awareness as wide as possible, like a wide angle lens on a camera, feeling deeply connected to the world I am in. I become part of the world that surrounds me. I do not think anything of what I perceive. I am only aware. I am exactly in the present. I think neither of the past nor of the future. If I think at all, I will not be in the present, but in past or future. Thus I must not think at all, if I expect to be only in the present.*

*Often I go walking places or pacing back and forth, and I frequently stop, thinking to myself, "What have I been thinking the past several minutes?" I have nothing to think about because I have no problems to solve. Often I have been walking around aware, but thinking little. Most of what I perceive, whether through seeing, hearing, smelling, or touching is not thought about.*

*If I perceive a sound, perhaps of my brother's voice, I recognize that the sound is familiar, but I do not think about the sound. If I thought about the sound, I would soon know that my brother had made the sound; and thinking more about it, I will know what he said. But if I never think about the sound, then I will not know that Kurt said it nor what he said, and not even that the sound was human or from an animal. I will only know that the sound is familiar, but it could be anything; just something I have heard a noise from before.*

*One of the dividing questions of Buddhism is "What is the best part of man, his head or his heart?" In other words, love and wisdom, which is more important? Is one more important or better than the other? I think love and wisdom are equally important parts of man. It is absurd to try to exclude parts of man's composition as unimportant. Even if one is more important, the short-sightedness of people leads to the exclusion of the less important, like winner versus loser. Man creates simple models of reality, but reality is not simple. Thus man's simple models of reality in many cases are inadequate. All models of the world are incomplete, and that's why they are only models, not replicas. Models will always be incomplete, and we will never fully know the world around us.*

*To make our ideas of reality simple for our finite minds, we exclude many things. Some believe the physical and mathematical model of reality, while others believe more simple models. Some believe that there exists a spiritual world, and that it is possible to create and destroy matter with the mind. But no one considers that perhaps all these things are true. Perhaps the powers of the spiritual world and the logical mathematical models of the physical world are both real and exist all around us.*

*In all cases, given propositions A, B, and C, consider the possibility of all three being true before deciding on mutual exclusion, that only one can be true.*

Brian's journal [December 14, 1989]

# BECOMING A NATURALIST
## Observations on a Siamese Cat

*Yesterday I held and cuddled a twenty-year-old Siamese cat. The interesting thing about the cat was its whine; it did not sound like a "meow," but like a little human baby crying. When I first heard the whine of this cat, I believed I actually heard a whining baby. The sound of the whine was on a vowel sounding like the "a" in "hat." The whine started sharply at a high volume and continuously declined in volume.*

*The time period of an average whine was about four or five seconds. The whine, once at its peak volume, decreases in volume fastest at the beginning of its decline, and its rate of decline slowly decreases. The pitch does not change as much but peaks at the same place as volume and has roughly the same shape. At any time the slope of the pitch has the same sign as that of the volume. If the volume is decreasing, so is the pitch. If the volume is increasing, then the pitch increases. The variation in pitch is smaller than that of the volume; that is, it is usually bounded by the latter.*

Brian's journal [July 4, 1989]

Brian exhibited a strong inclination toward becoming a naturalist. For that he had picked the right parents. Sue had been that way since early in childhood, having raised a young nestling and given shelter in her room to various other members of the animal kingdom at one time or another-much to the distress of her fastidious sister, who shared the room with Sue. I had brought with me from Germany the cocoon of a swallow-tail butterfly, which then emerged in the New World. Later I brought the egg case of a praying mantis into my room, only to have to deal with what seemed like hundreds of little praying mantises a few weeks later. So Brian was getting this from both sides.

A naturalist is a scientist whose primary tool is observational, and whose perspective is integrative. There has been a long-standing professional engagement in Europe with the domain of animal behavior. Jan Tinbergen and Konrad Lorenz come to mind. It appeared to me that an interest in "how nature behaves" came to be seen as an indispensable part of becoming a cultivated person. I had absorbed that early in my own family and had brought it with me. Sue modeled this as well, often spending long hours keying out plants while we were on hikes in the Santa Monica Mountains. This also came naturally to Brian. His observational skills were of course honed principally with regard to the quirks of his own nervous system.

## Scat Collection

*I collect scat. (Scat is a scientific word for animal feces.) I have collected bobcat scat, coyote scat, bear scat, rodent scat, and others. I collect for one of two purposes: (1) to identify the animal that I am tracking; (2) to understand the annual trend or cycle of animal's diet. I often pick up bobcat scat to see the size of the scat, and determine how different it is in size from a mountain lion scat. The variation of a coyote's diet is very interesting to me. I study the scat of different seasons. From insects, to berries, to rodents—this is how varied coyote scat is. They are omnivores.*

*Informing my roommates of this, they did not know what animal scat is. Once I defined it Terry, the chemistry major, looked shocked at the idea of collecting scat. Terry referred to scat as "shit," which is ambiguous. Nowadays anything can be referred to as "shit."*

*This evening I went to another town house, where Aaron (former prospective roommate) lives, and Terry often visits him. A girl there asked me: "Are you the one with the shit collection?" I answered yes. Soon afterwards, another guy present said, "I collect shit...cars, stereos..." The word "shit" is very ambiguous. It can represent anything, but connotes a disrespect for whatever it represents.*

*The moral of the story is that by using the word shit, Terry did not communicate to his friends what he intended to. "Animal feces" was the intended meaning of "shit," but a more global ambiguous meaning was perceived by the listeners.*

Brian's journal [September 17, 1989]

This nicely illustrates Brian's concreteness. I can just picture him committing all this faithfully to his journal in all seriousness. The same orientation toward objectivity infuses his observations of his fellow students as of the rest of nature.

The specific interest in scat came out of our long association with the Natural Science Section of the Sierra Club in Los Angeles, and with the Topanga Canyon Docents. Sue had been one of the three founders of the organization in 1973, and directed its activities until neurofeedback took over her life. This activity often took us into the mountains on hikes being led for the public or for school groups. The observational skills honed there were a good fit to Brian's natural inclinations. Unfortunately our nearest mammalian relatives around here lead mainly nocturnal lives, and so reveal themselves most obviously in their scat.

## Telepathy

*I am impressed by the correlation between what I visualize and what is communicated when practicing spiritual communication. What is communicated is dependent on how deeply everything was visualized. There exists no way to scientifically or objectively prove this, so I will make no such attempt to prove it. But the fact that this practice has never failed for me leads me to conclude that somehow my thoughts are perceived by the other person. Much of what I have experienced is inexplicable in physical terms. Therefore I regard this world of communication, ESP, and other spiritual communication as separate from the physical world.*

In a session with a group, we paired up, and each pair sat facing each other with legs crossed. Hands were held up, with the palms of one person against the palms of the other person, lightly making contact, not forceful. One person was a sender, the other a receiver. The sender and receiver both relaxed deeply, and blanked their minds before starting. Once both were relaxed, the sender started to deeply visualize some place or event. The receiver continued to maintain a blank mind. The receiver was expected to from time to time have something (thought) pop into his mind. The thought or image would hopefully be recollected later, but meanwhile he would blank his mind of any thoughts. The sender would give a gift before ending. There were five pairs of people during this practice, and communications were often transmitted to other receivers than the intended one.

During one visualization in which I was the sender, and my partner the receiver, I deeply visualized snow country in forested mountains, like that of the Teton Mountains in Wyoming, where I had been with NOLS. I visualized myself moving over the snow through pine trees, over rolling hills. I then visualized myself on the top of some peak, seeing for hundreds of miles in every direction. During this visualization, the *sense of moving over mountains—up and down—was more deeply visualized than the snow itself that transported me. I strongly recognized the trees which were around me, and the fact that it was cold, but the snow that surrounded me was not well recognized.*

*My partner had a vision of mountains with pine trees, and of moving over them. She had no concept that snow was part of it, or that I was pulling a sled, and that I had skis.*

*As a gift I thought so long of something organic, about the size of a baseball, but I wasn't sure what. Finally I gave her a rock, and with no visualization of the rock, or only a little. She received a pine cone. I only briefly thought of a pine cone. But I thought at length of some unknown object about the size of a baseball, and organic, and beautiful. The object was never defined in my mind, until I decided to forget that picture and give a stone.*

*The communication at all times corresponded to what I visualized, and not to what I actually thought about on an intellectual level.*

Brian's journal [August 17, 1989]

## Making Faces

*I have become so acutely aware of my mood. But I am not very aware of the expression on my face. During my first year with the EEG Biofeedback, I was for the first time happy. I smiled all the time so as to feel good. It was all for personal pleasure, but people understood it to mean I was glad to see them. I was really not at all aware of them, and if interrupted, I frowned.*

*My habit has changed. Now trying to be more relaxed, I tend not to raise my eyebrows as is natural when smiling. I smile but relax the eyebrows, and people think I am giving them an insincere smile. People smile insincerely back at me. I am conscious of my own expression 50% by how people respond to it.*

*Eventually the time will come when I do not need to make faces for personal benefit, and my expression will reflect what I feel towards the world.*

Brian's journal [August 18, 1989]

This passage illustrates just how much Brian had to manage consciously what for the rest of us proceeds more automatically. It also highlights what a functional right hemisphere accomplishes for us. Early in his life Brian had seemed to be on a normal path of development with regard to interaction with other people. This capacity was gradually lost as his neurological affliction became more manifest.

# FITFUL LURCHES TOWARD SOCIALIZATION
## *"Oth-Head"*

*Today I walked up to the Student Union building, and hiked in Poly Canyon. I saw several familiar faces from last year.*

*This evening I went to dinner at the cafe-teria, the "stalls," and on my way out saw Jim and Ralph in line. Ralph said to me on sight, "What's up 'OTH-HEAD'." That old nick-name that I despise was coined by my first roommate, Fred. They commented repeatedly on my scrag-gly face, due to my not having shaved this morn-ing. We exchanged a few words about what we did over summer. Jim said he saw my name in the newspaper,* The Mustang Daily. *He said my name was in the obituary section, and that Fred might have put it there. Fred works for* The Mus-tang Daily *as a printer, but not an editor. I did not see any obituary section in the newspaper, so I believe Jim lied to me.*

Brian's journal [September 17, 1989]

## *Sex and Complacency*

*Living with my roommate who held unchaste and*

*base beliefs, I found my own beliefs mildly affect-*
*ed by what he believed: that sex is the only real*
*pleasure in the world. I am often reminded of this*
*belief by both verbal and photographical means.*
*I believe that sex, if done often, can have the*
*effect of making one complacent or overly con-*
*tent, and reduce a person's awareness of the*
*outside world as he/she becomes more aware*
*inwardly of the sexual experiences.*

Brian's journal [September 17, 1989]

## Depression and Roommates

*Living with depression and with roommates*
*does not mix. Having depression, I must focus*
*on managing myself. Being so inwardly aware, I*
*appear to be self-centered. My roommate, Carl,*
*thinks I am self-centered; but so do many oth-*
*ers. Almost all my past roommates thought I was*
*self-centered. The reason for this is that I think*
*so much about myself and don't show much in-*
*terest in others. It follows that I also don't have*
*friends for this reason; I am too interested in*
*myself. But this inward interest is not toward my*
*normal desire; rather, it is toward the epileptic*
*and medication problem I live with. I am a rare*
*case; most people would not be so interested in*
*understanding themselves.*

Brian's journal [November 5, 1989]

Biofeedback makes physiology visible through instrumentation. But it can also be made accessible to us through strategies of enhanced awareness. Brian was always honing his skills of observation on his own physiology in order to enhance his level of control. Things shouldn't have to be this way. I believe it was Alfred North Whitehead who talked about consciousness as being like a small part of the brain where the light is on. The rest is just managing things out of sight and mind. What a shame to assign that small part of brain function where the light is on also to the task of managing our physiology. Well, this may not be the ideal, but that is what Brian felt he had to do. And it meant that he was not always good company.

It was in the traditional biofeedback world that an effort would usually be made to recruit the whole person into the task of self-regulation, whether through increased attention to the breath or to one's state of anxiety, or alertness, etc. This was not emphasized in neurofeedback because we don't particularly relate to our own EEG. Here the brain was just supposed to learn what it needed to learn and then let us go about our business.

Brian, on the other hand, actually could tell a great deal about the state of his brain at any moment, and that led him down a path of enhanced self-awareness to optimize his brain stability.

### Death Threats

*Tonight I saw* Pet Semetary *by Stephen King with roommates Carl and Steve. The movie is a great horror movie. After seeing much blood and gore, my roommate Carl threatened me with a steak knife with a blade 9 inches or longer. I was calm and took it as a joke. Carl is the only roommate who actually talks about killing me; and he sounds very serious.*

Brian's journal [November 18, 1989]

I am struck by the equanimity with which Brian treats the prospect of being killed by his roommate. Maybe it happens; maybe not. We'll see. That surely is a reflection of the tenor of chatter among college roommates. In an earlier day, such a threat would not have been considered benign. Now one cannot be sure. It strikes me as beyond doubt that the kinds of movies Brian was watching here have moved the dial in our society.

### Walking Target

*Around 6:30 p.m. today, some people were throwing Frisbees blindly and with significant force. First I saw one land 30 feet away from me. Then another flew only four feet above my head, and I ducked. I thought one of the people saw me, so I stopped paying attention to the people. I was walking up to the lighted street and out of the darkness of this side street. Then as I looked to my right, a Frisbee at lightning speed struck my chest right on the sternum. At first there was no abnormal response. About 3 seconds passed as I looked where the Frisbee came from. A person had shouted as the Frisbee hit me, then I felt a chill in my fingers. I shouted at the person who picked up the Frisbee. Rowdy people.*

Brian's journal [November 18, 1989]

Did Brian think he was being targeted with the Frisbee? I believe so. But his manner apparently stayed calm. This is so different from what might have happened even a year earlier. The chill he felt in his fingers is likely a protective physiological response to being hit in the chest.

## Social Awareness

*During the last few days since Monday I have had two midterm exams, and I registered for next quarter's classes, and I paid bills including a down payment on a twelve month lease here at Mustang Village. With so much going on—exams in particular—I expected to be stressed and possibly nervous. Instead I have been calm amidst every deed I have done. Through the week I have spoken with many people, usually just exchanging pleasantries. I am conversing more with students in my classes and with strangers outside. There is a general feeling that I am less "distant," that I am closer to the social atmosphere on campus, and that I am no longer an outside observer, but a participant in social activities. Somehow I am more a part of the student body, and less alienated.*

Brian's journal [February 5, 1990]

There is an expansion of social awareness here that for Brian represents a new departure. One could say that Brian has a well-developed "watcher self" that maintains constant vigilance over his actions, and now that watcher self is expanding its scope to include the interactions with others. This further development cannot be attributed to the neurofeedback training directly. Not much of that is happening any more. But the neurofeedback training made this possible.

It is common for people to experience further gains after they complete the neurofeedback sessions. This should not come as a surprise, and it should not exclude neurofeedback from the causal chain. As brain function is potentiated with the training, it will naturally progress on its own afterwards.

## Misconceptions

*Everyone has misconceptions, and they always will. The short-sightedness of people will remain. But the unwillingness of people to even consider that things may be different than they see them is astounding to me. My roommate (Carl) is convinced that I am psychotic and asexual; and he is unwilling to consider that I might not be psychotic.*

*People think they know from my expression what I am thinking. Especially impolite, but quite common, people think they know I am thinking about being laid. They like to think that I want the same things they want. But I don't. I have convinced Terry of that, and he has concluded that I am asexual. Others come to the conclusion that I must be homosexual.*

*Sometimes I am compelled to think about the things that many others have and I don't have. When I do this I become miserable with envy. What one thinks about is what he ends up wanting. If I think about women I will be upset that I don't have a girlfriend. So I focus on my studies and try to ignore all those things others have that I don't have.*

Brian's journal [February 6, 1990]

## BRAIN BALANCING
### Handwriting

*The quality of my writing is closely related to my EEG, or how well certain areas of my brain are functioning. It is a frequent occurrence, but a strange one, to see my signature and writing change form so that it looks like another person's writing. The way I am currently writing is the way I hope I will always write. The other way is hardly readable.*

*This evening I heard my father saying that writing is not taught as much in school as it should be. He believes this because of how difficult it is to read my brother's writing. I wish to add that I believe Kurt's writing could become better if he worked on the EEG machine some. I also know that this biofeedback has helped others with their writing.*

Brian's journal [September 1, 1989]

It is commonplace for us to have children in training who then comment on those of their classmates whom they regard as good candidates for neurofeedback as well. They have no problem picking them out, and they are probably right....

## Handedness

There are many factors that affect my brain chemistry and function every day; beliefs and the faculties of both hands are two factors I have been observing. There are two distinct types of faculties that often appear in separate hands, and especially for left-handed people. There is large-scale manual function, like throwing a ball, swinging a hammer or bat, or punching with a fist. There is small-scale or fine manual function of writing with a pen, or accurately placing the nail to hit with the hammer. For some people these two faculties are not in the same hand. Many left-handed people throw a ball with their right hand, while writing with their left. My father writes with his right hand and plays tennis with his left. But he is also very ambidextrous, and can throw with either hand.

When I chose to write with my left hand I felt like throwing a ball with my right. I have switched to being right-handed, and I am finding that I now feel like using my left for throwing a ball.

*Initially, when switching to right-handedness, I tried to do everything with my right. As a result, my brain started to feel out of balance, and my right brain was all upset because I ignored it too much. My left brain, meanwhile, was doing well, better than usual, except for a bad influence by the right brain.*

*By becoming aware of a split function of left and right hands, my brain felt more in balance. As my right hand develops more accuracy at fine work like writing, my left simultaneously feels more adapted to large-scale manual function. My hand remains poor at writing as long as my brain has this idea that either hand can be used for fine work.*

Brian's journal [September 6, 1989]

# THE INTEGRATED SELF
## Proper Breathing

*Breathing affects many aspects of physical be-havior, and coordination. When practicing stalk-ing, walking so slowly that movement is not discernible, with one step every two minutes, my balance and coordination is dependent on my focus on proper breathing. When eating, if I*

*breathe properly, it is natural that I do not inhale
my food. But if I expand my chest when I inhale,
moving my shoulders up and down as I breathe,
there is a tendency to inhale the food. When doing EEG Biofeedback or practicing relaxation,
breathing plays the largest role in making everything work. In books on the subject of Ninjitzu,
breathing properly is stressed very highly.*

*While walking in darkness, with eyes
closed, to the beat of a drum with one beat per
minute, my balance corresponded directly to my
awareness of both my center of gravity and my
breathing. Both my breathing and my center of
gravity felt strongly bound like a unit and were
both equally important in maintaining balance.
Breathing inflates the body and modifies its
form. One must be aware of his breathing or else
the change in form caused by inhaling will make
him lose his balance. To breathe only in the
abdomen is better because the modification in
body form is reduced. The smaller the change is,
the less the body needs to move to compensate
for the change. Breathing in the chest also results in a higher center of gravity than breathing
in the abdomen.*

*In myself and others, proper breathing is a key
part of making the EEG instrument work when
doing biofeedback. A Highland Hall student said,*

*"It is all breathing," when I asked him how he kept the light on.*

*Breathing both induces and suppresses epileptic seizures. My first epileptic seizure was caused by holding my breath. All other seizures I have had started with hyperventilation. Calm, relaxed breathing suppresses risk of seizure. Hyperventilation is the first sign of a seizure. Hyperventilation goes along with emotional excitement. When there is hyperventilation and emotional excitement a seizure is almost certain to occur, unless the emotional excitement is suppressed. But if the hyperventilation is deliberate, and not emotionally induced, then I am calm emotionally and a seizure is not apt to occur.*

Brian's journal [August 18, 1989]

When a reward structure is set up as in EEG biofeedback, one will use whatever means are available to reach the objective. So is a breathing strategy counter-productive in what we are trying to accomplish? In one sense, moving toward more relaxed breathing helps to move one to the desired calm state that facilitates higher scoring in the feedback. So it is helping to move the person in the right direction. In another sense, one might say that the whole point is to get to the goal by means of altered brain activity, not by manipulating the breath.

In actuality, there is not a conflict. If a person scores more by virtue of a breathing strategy, the biofeedback system simply alters the goal to keep the level of challenge reasonably constant. So in this case, there is no free lunch. When I first did my own training, however, I found that my EEG was of such low amplitude that I rarely exceeded the reward threshold even at its most sensitive setting. By the mere expedient of turning my head slightly, I generated enough muscle tension in my neck that I was able to score more consistently. That wasn't doing me any good, but then I was not aware for some time that I was actually turning my head. All this was happening beneath consciousness. My brain knew that the object was to score points, and it found out how to get them by trial and error. I had been undergoing very expensive training of muscle tension in my neck! This inappropriate reward of muscle tension has since been barred with a high-frequency inhibit.

## Incredible Changes

*The kinds of changes that have been occurring are drastic and incredible from my viewpoint. Communicating to others what these changes are is difficult. Here I will describe the course of changes since the summer of 1989, or some of them, those changes which are most important.*

*At the beginning of last summer I was doing well with my sleep after tolerating my roommate's habits. But arriving back home, I soon messed up my perfect sleep by missing my medicine, and a few days later I had a seizure. I did not recover quickly from the effects of the seizure. More than a month later, in the beginning of August, I went to a tracking workshop. During this workshop we practiced meditation, stalking, and track identification. The meditation and stalking were most beneficial because they helped my mind and body control. I continued to practice meditating and stalking after the workshop; combined with stretching, I kept myself quite well.*

*During the month of August I hit my head twice; once on the forehead, and once on the back. Much delta frequency showed up in my EEG, and it also caused much dizziness. But this would not last more than a month's time; I had expected this, and it came true. My EEG was doing well except for the effects of the head injury. Since I knew, from past experience, that going to school boosted my EEG, I predicted with some certainty that I would experience a miraculous change at school. This miraculous change has occurred, and I am down to 400mg of Tegretol because of this change. But it is not the Tegretol reduction which is miraculous. I have eliminated from my life the mental state which put me under risk of a seizure, and have felt another strengthening of my right-handedness. This miraculous change—it does not appear from these words to be miraculous—has affected my focus on school.*

*I expect future changes to be similar but possibly not so drastic as this. But "drastic" only refers to the rate of change. When such change is accomplished quickly, it is drastic, but this change could also occur more slowly. After this miraculous change, I feel certain that I am going to get off my medicine. I immediately decided to go down from 600mg, and have gone down to 400mg.*

*In the future I will go down further on my medicine, but this will not happen until I devote more time to changing myself (beliefs, feelings, thoughts). Because I live on medicine, I am not emotionally who I would be if I were not on the medicine, or "mind-altering drug." This medicine, like an illegal drug, modifies the way I think and feel. I will not be who I know I really am until I get off the medicine.*

*It is very important that I follow through on my "temporary life goal." As long as I am taking Tegretol, I will not be my true self, and I am thus not fit to do many things in the world. Nothing is done as well as I could do it were I not on the medicine. Thus I do not want to take on most responsibilities in life until I am off the medicine. When I do get off the medication, I will have my self-confidence back.*

Brian's journal [November 24, 1989]

## Integration

*I must follow a path of integrating my mind, body, and spirit. The spirit is more abstract, and mind and body are more what I am focusing on. Although I still must integrate all of them; in delving into the depths of the "self" I must consider all parts of the self. Mind and body are not whole without the spirit. If one of these three parts is in bad shape, it will influence badly the other two.*

*My mind was once separate, as two halves, but I have integrated it together. What is left is the mind's control of the body, and the body's control of emotion and mind. Mind and body should exist as one; they both affect each other. The EEG biofeedback works only on the mind; thus it does not work on integrating the mind and the body. What is most important now is the time I find to be alone and to focus on understanding my "self."*

Brian's journal [December 7, 1989]

EEG biofeedback brings awareness of physiological states that we are not generally sensitive to. Once such awareness is developed, then EEG biofeedback is optional. Indeed, most of what has been accomplished with biofeedback using our "Western" scientific instrumentation has been accomplished without it by yogis from time immemorial: control of mental states, heart rate and metabolic rate, hand temperature, etc.

I suggested to Brian that his extensive awareness of his brain had a lot to do with the problems he was having. An analogy may serve: if one's cross country skis have ice on the bottom, one knows exactly where the ice is. If there is no ice on them, one knows nothing about the bottom of one's skis. I thought that Brian's awareness of his brain would diminish as his brain function improved. Much later, Brian reminded me of this conversation, and said that that was becoming true.

## SEIZURES AND SLEEP
### Relaxed Focus

*Sleeping properly is essential to maintaining a good EEG. When one is tired, his EEG will not look as good as it normally does, and will be partially composed of more slow wave (or theta and delta) than would normally be so. When I go to bed I must still have mental energy left so that I can come to a relaxed focus with sufficient sensorimotor rhythm (SMR)—12 15Hz activity—in my EEG. Getting into this relaxed focus, I stay awake for at least a period of 15 minutes, but often am awake for an hour.*

*The goal of the focus is to be aware of my body enough so that I eliminate the possibility of any unintentional movement. The goal also includes getting as much rest as possible, but that does not mean falling asleep. Being as relaxed as possible, often I have been awake for more than an hour, and on one occasion, with company in the room, I was awake for five hours. Despite this, I was still rested up after eight hours in bed.*

*I use this method of sleeping mostly to prevent seizures. By doing this "relaxed focus" every night, I have been able to cope with people poking me, playing music, yelling, conversing, and partying beside my bed with no seizures.*

Brian's journal [July 10, 1989]


### Workouts and Seizures

*During the 7th I had also gone for a workout in the weight room on campus. It was muscular strength exercises that contributed greatly to seizures when I was young, and this is still true now. I felt like I was a little more susceptible directly after the workout, so I rested, meditated (30 minutes), and finally was able to get up feeling good again. But this workout could haunt me later. Since I did not meditate before sleep, I experienced a restlessness in the muscles which were worked most.*

*No seizures, good sleep; it pays to be aware of myself and do the right thing before it is too late.*

Brian's journal [October 8, 1989]

Brian is observing the profound effect of physical exertion on arousal level, which apparently put him at risk of seizure. Most likely the rate of change of arousal level after the exercise is the issue, something that is also observed with migraine. For example, it is much more likely that someone gets a migraine two or three hours after a tennis match than during the period of exertion.

## Aborting Seizures

*During the last year I have seen a gradual change in severity of seizures. One year and a half ago I was still experiencing many intense motor seizures, seizures in which I had clenched fists and was injuring myself and damaging things around me. I would often wake up with cuts and bruises after a seizure. It also took me a few days to recover. I would experience a loss of coordination and loss of speech. My speech would be unclear. My ability to walk would be impaired for a few hours after the seizure. These types of seizures were worst two years ago. They were around for about 8 months.*

*My motor seizures around the summer of 1988 were beginning to become less severe. But they still involved much muscular tension and hyperventilation.*

*Around January 1989 I started to experience seizures in which I would instantly abort the seizure by yelling "NO!" and a sleepwalking state of consciousness would follow. The amount of motor control lost was decreasing. The consequences the following day were less severe. The seizures typically occurred at night between 12:00 a.m. and 2:00 a.m. I was living with a roommate who always had his television on. He enjoyed seeing me have seizures.*

*Ever since the winter and spring of 1989, my seizures have been becoming less and less severe. My motor control during a seizure is becoming greater. There is less tension in a seizure. I am more loose and relaxed. Hyperventilation is not as intense. Much of all this change is due to proper breathing.*

Brian's journal [October 13, 1989]

Brian discovered his ability to abort seizures, just as many others in his position have done. The techniques generally involve changes in arousal level, and an active assertion of control. This is the very opposite of an attitude of victimization and dependency, of utter helplessness before fate, which neurologists implicitly promote with their epileptic patients by framing the issue entirely within the medical model. The medications target one aspect of the seizure risk, namely the excitability of neuronal membranes. But we know that seizure incidence is highly context-sensitive. This is best understood at the level of the whole neural network rather than at the level of the synapse. We are in a position to influence network stability directly, with behavioral measures over the short term, and with neurofeedback training over the long term.

It is somewhat puzzling to see Brian referring to a sleepwalking state of consciousness, because normally people do not have recall of such states. But we have a collective history of under-estimating the variability among sleep states. Brian was experiencing partial loss of motor control along with at most partial loss of consciousness. It is not surprising, in retrospect, that his sense of increasing mastery over this quasi-seizure phenomenon gave him confidence that he was on the path to mastering his medical challenge entirely on his own.

The fact that these kinds of quasi-seizures were such a large preoccupation for him at this time was unknown to us. I'm sure Brian felt that if he told us all that was going on we would have pressured him to take another look at medical remedies. And in that judgment he would have been correct!

## Interrupted Sleep

*Immediate interruption of sleep or rest, when in a semi-conscious state of awareness, to go to the bathroom or do anything that requires getting out of bed, may change the way I sleep the rest of the night, so that I wake up feeling like I had a bad sleep. I am not fully conscious when I decide it is time to get up and go to the toilet in the night. My mind may be conscious but I am physically relaxed. If I interrupt my rest by getting out of bed and walking to the bathroom while I am well relaxed, then I feel like I am in a sleepwalking state of consciousness. Once I make it back to my bed, I am no longer feeling as good as I felt before I left. Afterwards my body, especially the limbs, are no longer relaxed, and my brain is in confusion. I believe I am more susceptible to a seizure after interrupting my sleep in the night than when I went to bed initially.*

*Every night I carefully take the time to become relaxed before going to sleep, so that I prevent seizures. I should do the same thing after interrupting my sleep in the night. It is only necessary if I rob my limbs of their relaxation period by getting out of bed. Conscious or unconscious, it is not important as long as I am relaxed and I do not move or use my limbs. The more I move my arms and legs in the night, the worse I feel the following morning.*

*The next time I wake up in the night to go to the bathroom, I should stretch my limbs before getting out of bed. I must wake myself slowly just as I put myself into relaxation and sleep slowly.*

Brian's journal [September 8, 1989]


### Sleep Positions

*I would never have guessed that lying in bed with the arms and legs straight and close together was conducive to better sleep. But all experiences I have had of good deep sleep have been in this position.*

Brian's journal [February 13, 1990]

---

*Different sleeping positions help to relax different muscles in the body. Depending on what muscles are tense, a different choice of position may be taken. Last night I found the position of lying on my stomach rather unrelaxing. But when I lie sideways in the fetal position I could rest well.*

Brian's journal [February 23, 1990]

*What position a person sleeps in is a function of the distribution of tension within his body. This tension is mostly involuntary muscular tension, but there may be tension of voluntary muscles. The distribution of tension during sleep is closely related to the distribution of tension during the day. One's physical state during sleep affects his physical state during the daytime, and vice versa.*

Brian's journal [March 4, 1990]

### Cycles

*Last night I slept badly right after the best sleep I have had in a long time. The cycle is that after a bad sleep, my sleep slowly gets better for about 4 weeks (approx. a month) until I reach a night of superb sleep. Then the next night I sleep so badly that a seizure may result and the cycle starts all over. With this cycle I had one seizure around the start of January, another in early February, and now finally a bad sleep in March. This time I just slept with headache but no seizure.*

*The solution to this problem is to be even more disciplined. Do whatever helps sleep, every day, even if I feel great. Stretch, meditate, exercise in equal magnitudes, independently of how I feel. Keep study time in good proportion whether feeling good or bad. So do not stretch when I feel the need, plan it ahead of time and do it as planned without regard to whether I feel great or not.*

*Next quarter will be more disciplined like this.*

Brian's journal [March 14, 1990]

## DIET AND ALCOHOL

*My roommate Carl has been inspired by the fact that today is my 21st birthday. He has been talking about buying a lot of liquor and getting me drunk. We now have a liquor bar.*

*Last night I had a little Peppermint Schnapps, and was informed that if I wished to stay down here in the living room, I had to drink. I refused to have anything more because I just went from 600mg to 500mg dosage of Tegretol. I must be very careful or else I will have a seizure.*

Brian's journal [October 7, 1989]

---

*Last night I experienced a seizure. During the preceding 6 hours I had some paprika, and a half a can of beer. Paprika and alcohol both contribute to seizures. I am unsure which of these two constituents contributed most to the seizure.*

*The alcohol did not take effect until after I was in bed. Paprika always has an immediate effect. Josh (roommate) said the alcohol would probably not take effect until a few hours later.*

*During the evening I did the following: Around 7:30 p.m. I had a touch of dip with paprika in it. Around 8:40 p.m. I left in the car with Josh and friends to Farmers' Market on Higuera. Josh and I were dropped off at a nearby friend's house. Renee (friend), Josh, and I went up Higuera Street where Farmers' Market was still happening, and eventually arrived at the Bar. We went into the bar, and there was a jazz band playing in there. Josh was drinking a beer. I had a coke, and later had a little alcohol. I still felt totally safe from any seizures. The time period I was in the bar was approximately 9:30 p.m. to 10:45 p.m. I walked home, and arriving back at Mustang Village at 11:05 p.m. I soon went to bed. I still felt resistant to any seizures. I started to doubt my resistance to seizure even though I did not feel anything. The question now is what caused me to become susceptible? There are several possibilities.*

*(1) The alcohol took effect about 12:30 p.m. when I started feeling susceptible.*

*(2) My fear or doubt about being resistant to seizure made me susceptible.*

*(3) My medication, which I took around 11:30 p.m. started to interfere with the alcohol which caused a seizure.*

*Before 12:30 p.m., I had been in bed for one hour and fifteen minutes. During this time, I had been resting deeply and felt safe from any seizure. I believe I probably slept a little bit during that time, and I was well relaxed for the duration of it. But then I woke up still feeling good, I mean I came out of my deep relaxation. I started to wonder why I am not susceptible. So I started to do some different things that soon made me susceptible. I think it was what I believed last night that influenced the seizure. It was one factor in causing it.*

*This morning I had no recollection of a seizure. A slight headache and a sheet and blanket pulled off the bed suggested something to me. I asked my roommate, Carl, if anything happened last night.*

*He answered, "Yes, you did a three-sixty (360 degrees) on the bed and fell perfectly on the floor."*

*Steve continued with, "If you ever have a seizure again I will not get up unless you start dismantling your computer, then maybe I will get up."*

*Let's get back to talking about possible caus-
es of the seizure. I think that possibilities one
and three are different. In the first possibility I am
considering the effect of alcohol directly on my
brain. In the third I am considering the possible
conflict between alcohol and Tegretol. I am under the impression that it is the alcohol conflict-
ing with the Tegretol which caused the seizure,
that alcohol has a reduced effect on seizures
when anticonvulsants are not present.*

Brian's journal [October 13, 1989]

Brian talks so matter-of-factly about his seizures, and at this point he
even talks about being able to predict their occurrence within a given
night. At a minimum, he knew when he was vulnerable. This was all
news to us until we got to see Brian's journal. He was like the mountain
climber who had finally left his instructor behind. He was on his own
in figuring out the route to the top. He knew that if we'd had the whole
picture we would have gone into action one way or another, and he
clearly did not want that.

### No More Alcohol

*The seizure that occurred on the night of Thurs-
day, October 12 was minor, but like with any
seizure there were ensuing effects. I was more
unfocused today. I felt less clear in my thinking.
I almost decided to tell my chemistry lab teacher
that I was epileptic to explain my confusion and
being the last one to finish the lab.*

*The effects the seizure had on me resembled sleepwalking transitions of thought more than the effects of motor seizures. Sleepwalking worsens my ability to focus. Motor seizures also affect focus, but they mess up coordination and balance as well. My seizures are no longer affecting my coordination and balance, but they do affect my awareness and how I think. I am finding myself day-dreaming briefly or going off on tangents.*

*The consequences of the seizure will not be around for long. I shall recover from this soon. My emotional uptightness was also present today, but that should disappear also.*

*If I wish to be mentally on the competitive edge as well as physically, then I must stop intoxicating myself with alcohol.*

*NO MORE ALCOHOL BRIAN!*

*NO MORE INTOXICATION!*

*Say this to your roommate T.F. who keeps encouraging you to drink. Don't ever drink a little alcohol. Drink NO alcohol at all. NO TASTING!*

Brian's journal [October 16, 1989]

## *Peppermint Schnapps*

*Last night I had a light bite of cake with peppermint schnapps. I think this cake contributed to a feeling of the breathing symptoms of a seizure. I did not sleep well as a result of this. But I have no idea whether a seizure actually occurred. This bad sleep last night is due either to the peppermint schnapps or to my discontinuance of stretching and meditation. Stretching and meditation help boost my seizure threshold by promoting better breathing and body awareness.*

Brian's journal [November 17, 1989]

It is noteworthy that we find Brian unable to pass up alcohol after vowing to leave it alone, for which he had good reason. He never speaks of craving alcohol. He doesn't even tell of getting a positive reaction from drinking it. There is just the normal kind of curiosity, plus in this case a lot of social pressure. And yet that was sufficient to override his best judgment.

If one imagines someone not only feeling good with drinking alcohol but also craving it, just how likely is it that willpower will win out? We have a rationalizing mind going up against a determined brain. That is an unfair contest. It is only too likely that the brain will have its way, and that is what we generally observe. Just as it was wrong to give Brian only the behavioral model in which to understand his deviant behavior, it is wrong to frame the problem of drug abuse as primarily a moral failing and a failure in self-control. Even if it does not start out as a brain-based problem, it soon becomes one. Brian's history can be seen as a paradigm for so many who are contending against brain-based disorders, all with precious little help either from the field of medicine or from society at large.

## Paprika

*Last night Josh, Terry, Dan, and I had a pot-luck with guests. Some of the food was quite heavily dosed with paprika. I ate a lot of it, thus I put a lot of paprika into my system. I also did a little weight training yesterday; I worked only on my legs and abdominals. When I went to bed I experienced a strange pain in my forehead, specifically the temporal regions on both sides. The pain was not like the pressure (which is not painful) that I typically experience from Tegretol or being excited. Pressure would always keep me in a wakeful state so I didn't sleep. But these streaks of pain did not possess a wakeful pressure. When I increased my level of consciousness the pain disappeared. But with a decrease in consciousness there had to be a corresponding degree of tension in the shoulders and solar plexus to eliminate the pain. The better I could focus my breathing abdominally and release tension from above, the better and happier I slept. I slept quite well, apparently, but during the night I wondered whether I would.*

Brian's journal [March 4, 1990]

## MEDICATION

*Some people take Tegretol only in the evening once a day, others spread their dosage out over the course of the day. I have been advised in the past to take it about three times a day. When I have been under a lot of stress and had frequent seizures, I am more dependent on the Tegretol, and I take it five or six times a day. Currently my need for Tegretol has been so negligible that I have not felt any need for it, and only take it for safety. In every case I take the same dosage per day, either all at once, or broken into little pieces.*

*When my need is great for Tegretol, the Tegretol gives me a boost and helps me. When I do not feel like I need it, the Tegretol fogs my mind and I don't think as clearly. The Tegretol in each case pulls me to a fixed level.*

*I have found it beneficial to take my medicine all at once in the evening before bed, delaying it as long as possible. Since the Tegretol fogs my thinking, I take it when I decide I no longer need to think clearly. So it is usually not until I am in my P.J.s and getting in bed that I take it.*

*Since I do not take Tegretol in the morning, my mind is not fogged during the day and my thinking actually peaks out in the afternoon and evening. The effect of the Tegretol I took before bed is still present in the morning. I am also a morning person. My mind is usually freshest at this time. So around early afternoon when the medicine's effect is weaker, but I am still full of thinking powers, my focus and ability to complete homework is best. In the evening I feel even better often in respect to draining my brain of Tegretol. But I am not as full of energy for studies by the evening, so I concentrate on athletic activities.*

*By only taking medicine in the evening, I drug my brain only when the medicine is crucial, and that is at night while I'm asleep.*

*The task that best shows me where I stand with respect to being foggy or clear-minded is the task of reading and assimilating in depth what I read. I can read any time of day. But when my mind is foggy, words go right through my mind without my registering what they mean. When I am clear-minded I follow the meaning behind the text much better, and more quickly. When I am foggy, I find myself reading every sentence at least twice slowly to understand it. I am discovering how I can be like many others who have little trouble with fourteen units in school. This*

*clear thinking was something that I experienced*
*rarely, like once a month last year. Now I expe-*
*rience it at least every other day at maximum*
*power, and even on the in-between days.*
Brian's journal [October 7, 1989]

Brian had chosen a path in which mental clarity is crucial, and yet his experience of it could be so fleeting. Trying to relate this to my own life experience, the analogy that comes to mind is that of illness. When one is physically ill, the brain is otherwise occupied, and one's mental resources are just not available. Finding myself in such circumstances, I would still try to press on with one thing or another, and there would come a point where I'm reading paragraphs twice to understand them, just as Brian is describing. I would then capitulate and decide that I just need to let my body recover. For Brian, there is no such respite. This is his perpetual reality.

*As I become less dependent on Tegretol, the*
*side effects of depression, and motor tics are*
*becoming more apparent. Seizures cause para-*
*noia and loss of motor coordination. In the midst*
*of paranoia, the side effect of depression was*
*not noticeable. With little motor control due to*
*seizures, a few motor tics would go unnoticed.*
*I had assumed every little thing was due to*
*the seizures.*

*Every day my thoughts are full of resentment,*
*feelings of sadness or despair. But these feel-*
*ings are confronted by my "will." I use my will-*
*power to redirect my feelings and hopefully have*
*favorable interactions with people. Paranoia no*

*longer burdens me; it is gone. But the depressing effect of Tegretol continues. Tegretol depresses me in the morning when I wake up. Late in the day when almost 24 hours have passed since I last took my medicine, I am more open to humor. I become filled with humor. Most of the time I am depleted of humor. Tegretol "flattens" me. My emotional self is hidden behind so much fog by the Tegretol. To flatten or dampen my emotions was appropriate when I was full of anger. Now it is bad.*

*I thought myself to be a morning person. Certainly I still am, but it often feels the other way around because my mind goes off on tangents. The Tegretol is known to cause confusion as a side effect. I believe I am noticing that effect. Early in the day my mind wandered frequently off on tangents. Later in the day my focus becomes better.*

*Over the last few years of school, whenever I have experienced periods of perfect concentration (about one hour's worth), it was when my medicine had slackened off, and it was almost time to take it again. These experiences always occurred about the time that I took my evening medicine, but before I took it.*

Brian's journal [October 24, 1989]

Brian is describing a very interesting phenomenon here. When one symptom dominates, others may go unnoticed. If the masking symptom were not present, the other symptoms would get our full attention. That same phenomenon is operative on the attending professional, whose attention is likewise drawn to the most serious symptoms in the hierarchy of distress. But then that tends to create another problem, that of diagnostic tunnel vision. Once the principal issue is labeled, other issues just get crowded off the stage. In Brian's case, it was the diagnosis of epilepsy that framed not only our understanding but that of the professionals. Observations are shaped by expectations, so a narrow focus can develop in which one looks for evidence that is supportive of the chosen diagnosis, and one also tends to either dismiss or diminish evidence that lies outside of the template.

At one point we listed all of the conditions in the Diagnostic Statistical Manual of Psychiatry (the DSM-IV) for which Brian met the diagnostic criteria, and we came up with twelve. The neurological diagnosis of epilepsy makes it thirteen in total. Any one of these diagnoses would have taxed the skills of any mental health professional, and yet none of them were up for discussion because epilepsy had become the defining issue. Everything else was seen in refraction from that diagnostic lodestone.

*Day after day, I am feeling ever less dependent on Tegretol. Thus the positive effects of Tegretol are no longer felt. I now feel only the negative effects: depression, mental confusion, motor tics, and dizziness. Last night all these negative side effects were felt so strongly, I became eager to rid my mind of this drug.*

*As the night wore on (7 p.m. to 10:30 p.m.) my mind became more clear. Every few minutes my mind felt clearer than before. This happens every night: my thinking continuously becomes more clear. This night was so good that the intensity of the side effects felt unbearable.*

*By the time bedtime (11:00 p.m.) rolled around, I was feeling incredibly clear in my thoughts, and physically in great control. Because of the observed side effects of Tegretol, I chose to go without my medicine until I would later feel a need for it. I went two hours without feeling any need for the medicine. But meanwhile I did not get sleep, although I was well relaxed. I then decided to take 300mg to possibly help me sleep. It helped significantly. I was soon asleep (1:00 a.m.). Three hours later, 4:00 a.m., I woke up with a big headache. I took another 100mg, hopefully this would help the headache by adjusting the chemical imbalance in my brain. I later took 200mg more Tegretol, and in another hour the headache disappeared. I woke up in the morning around 8:30 a.m. feeling well. The headache I had in the night was due to Tegretol deficiency. It is distinctly different from a headache resulting from seizure. The headache was sharp and painful, while a seizure headache is dizziness and unfocused.*

*The result of all this experimentation has been an increased focus today. Although I took 600mg total of Tegretol, I am not experiencing intense effects from Tegretol. I think the Tegretol is not having much of an effect because it was taken so sporadically.*

Brian's journal [October 25, 1989]

---

*The variations in my mental processes due to variations in levels of Tegretol during the last few days have been bizarre. Each day I take my medicine before bed. Afterwards, the effect of the Tegretol slowly declines over the next 24 hours. This decline in Tegretol level, combined with a superior mental state, causes many of the side effects of Tegretol to become evident. I am experiencing auditory-visual hallucinations, motor tics, mood alterations, and dizziness.*

*Three nights ago I attempted to go without my medicine. I had a seizure. Only choking and gasping with short breaths; no motor seizure. The body was relaxed while choking was occurring. During the next day, my EEG was doing superior. But the following day after that (Thursday), my EEG has started to be low in my left brain. This initial up before a down is very strange to follow a seizure. Usually I have a down directly after a seizure. But here I had a whole day doing superior before things got worse the following day.*

*Today I am still experiencing the after-effects of the seizure.*

*Tegretol becomes very difficult to tolerate when my brain is doing superbly well. This is so because many of the side effects start to manifest themselves. I also feel like the Tegretol is only hindering my thoughts and in no way helping. Getting off Tegretol is a journey in tolerating depression and dizziness. Depression and dizziness are the most difficult of the side effects to tolerate.*

*I am finding it difficult to focus on school in the midst of this problem with Tegretol, and the realization that it is actually possible I will get off Tegretol.*

Brian's journal [October 27, 1989]

---

*On the night of November 11, I went to bed with a total of 330mg of Tegretol. I went to bed at 9:45 p.m. and felt good. But I never could dream. As deeply relaxed as I would get, I never entered REM sleep. It felt like something was missing which needed to be there for REM sleep to occur. This experience is my third experience of an inability to dream when I go under 400mg of Tegretol.*

*During last night my body and mind felt perme-*
*ated throughout by the SMR which prevents sei-*
*zures. I felt deeply relaxed and ready for sleep.*
*Any outside observer would think I was asleep,*
*but I was conscious. From 9:45 until 4:00 a.m.*
*I was conscious. At 4:00 a.m. I took the other*
*70mg of Tegretol. I wanted to make certain that*
*I at least had a couple hours of "dream" sleep.*

*For months I have used meditation to build up*
*my seizure threshold. Often before bed I spend*
*half an hour meditating. While meditating one*
*feels aware and that he will not fall into sleep. In*
*meditation the body can become as relaxed as in*
*sleep, but the mind stays subtly aware. So also*
*in my sleep (or deep rest) last night. My body*
*was deeply relaxed, but my mind stayed aware.*
*Meditation has become my model for sleep*
*without seizures. This seems to suggest that I*
*will not "dream."*

Brian's journal [November 12, 1989]

---

*Today is the 31st of December 1989. Tomor-*
*row is the start of a new decade. The time is*
*10:00 a.m. I look forward to the new year with*
*hope. Next quarter at Cal Poly—starting January*
*3rd—I hope to devote my energy totally towards*
*school, and less towards health like last quarter.*

*I am taking 300mg of Tegretol. Three weeks ago I was taking 400mg. Adjusting to 300mg has involved an increased awareness of the body, and a decreased awareness of the brain. Every night in bed I say to myself "you are body, you have no mind." I must sustain a vivid sensation of all body parts (ambulatory body parts), and have no awareness of the existence of a head. I vividly feel the back of my neck, but nothing above that. Every time I try to analyze how my brain is doing, my EEG gets worse with delta waves in my forebrain, causing headache.*

Brian's journal [December 31, 1989]

---

*During the Christmas holiday I experienced a lot of headaches as a result of a transition from 400mg to 300mg of Tegretol. Now back at school, I no longer feel like I have too little medicine, but too much. Before, during the headaches, I felt an emptiness in my head. Now, feeling too overloaded with medication, I am foggy and feel too much pressure inside my head (often with dizziness).*

*Feeling foggy from too much medication is a result of how I spread my dosage out over the day more so than the actual dosage I take. Taking 100mg in the morning, 100mg in the afternoon, and 100mg before bed, I am kept fuzzy and fogged in the mind all day. This keeps the level of Tegretol consistently the same, and is the primary reason for spreading it out. Bunching up the dosage to 300mg at bedtime creates a drastic differential over time: I am extremely fuzzed right after taking the medication, and more headaches and side effects from the medicine are usually experienced the next day.*

Brian's journal [January 10, 1990]

---

*My medicine or my epileptic seizure exactly one week ago: one or both of these has contributed to a feeling of anger and sadness with a pessimistic outlook. I have been rather ugly-looking with my sad, angry face. But I only experience the feeling on a subconscious level, no thoughts are associated with the feeling most of the time. Thoughts are only involved when I am experiencing an impulse of paranoia towards someone who has glanced at me, or towards something else.*

*I have also slept poorly the last four nights. I go to bed around 11:00 p.m. to get up at 7:00 a.m. the next day. I do not fall asleep until past midnight, usually after 1:00 a.m. I am drowsy and grumpy most of the next day, until the late evening when I again feel energetic before bed.*

*I believe my medicine has an influence on this. I am currently taking 300mg before bed, and that is it. My thinking is clearest before I take my medicine at 11:00 P.M.*

Brian's journal [January 18, 1990]

---

*For the duration of Winter Quarter 1990 I was on 300mg of Tegretol per day. I started to go down ever so slightly two days before finals week. By the time I was done with Finals week and in Washington, D.C. I was taking about 280mg per day. I did some biofeedback on the new filter, which inhibits 22-30 Hz. Inhibiting this high beta improved my sleep significantly and immediately.*

*I dropped down to 200mg per day in 3 days. I had taken two days to go from 280mg to 250mg per day, but this felt no different to me so I straight away dropped to 200mg per day. There was a large spike of delta appearing on my EEG power spectral density. Dropping to 200mg per day was a large drop and would take some adjustment. Thursday, March 29 was my first day on 200mg I noticed results the next day. Thursday night I had slept well, but Friday night I did not sleep perfectly, and I got a cold. Sunday I took Greyhound back to San Luis Obispo. I did not feel well during Sunday. I experienced a lot of headaches. My headache and illness only got worse at school. So Tuesday I went back up to 300mg per day to help eliminate the delta activity that gave me the headache. Delta does not give me seizures but it can make one ill. I may not be able to study/think without a certain degree of high beta (20 to 30 Hz) in my EEG. This means I will not be able to go below some level of Tegretol. That is for the duration of this quarter (Spring). When Summer rolls around I will be training and expect to get off my medicine.*

*I had shut myself out of life. But I am re-entering. To shut oneself out is to be miserable; to enter into life is to be happy.*

Brian's journal [April 6, 1990]

---

*Since the Friday of "dead week" Winter Quarter, I have been going down on my medicine. The night of March 16th I had started to scrape a slight bit of Tegretol off my bedtime dosage. A few days later I scraped it off my 3:00 p.m. dosage rather than my evening dosage. I was taking 300mg daily, divided into three dosages: 100mg at 7:00 a.m., 100mg at 3:00 p.m., 100mg at 10:00 p.m. (my bedtime). I kept scraping off the Tegretol, and made them very small for the duration of final's week.*

*On March 24, Saturday, I left on an airplane to Washington, D.C. I met my family at the "Ramada Renaissance Techworld" in downtown Washington, D.C. I spent Sunday through Tuesday touring Washington with Kurt. We visited museums and monuments.*

Brian's journal [April 22, 1990]

We attended the national biofeedback conference in Washington, D.C., in March of 1990, to exhibit our instrumentation. For the first time, we were exhibiting Brian's software for the Amiga computer. Brian flew in from San Luis Obispo to join us. He spent the week rooming with Kurt, and sight-seeing in Washington. This experience cemented their relationship in a wonderful way.

In the fall of 1989 we had met with Barry Sterman and his wife Lorraine at our house in Sherman Oaks. He told us of the usefulness of a filter for the higher EEG frequencies to inhibit activity related to muscle tension, anxiety, etc. We added that feature to the software, and Brian was one of the first to benefit from that addition. This was the first of many changes that were to be made from the original program. In nearly every case, giving the brain a little more information about itself, albeit selectively, was additive to the overall effect.

*I also found time to get hooked up to a new filter on the EEG Biofeedback machine. The new filter inhibited high beta (22 Hz to 30 Hz). Reducing the high beta increased the SMR and I slept significantly better. I started to drop to 250mg per day on Monday. The drop to 250mg seemed so unnoticeable on Tuesday that on Wednesday I dropped my dosage all the way to 200mg per day. My mind felt empty and free of thought. It was recuperating from the stress of finals week one week earlier.*

*During Thursday and Friday I felt o.k. on 200mg per day but there continued to be a lot of delta present in my EEG. Friday night I had not slept too well and experienced even more delta. The delta became somewhat painful, but a little bit of headache from delta was always a nice alternative to the fuzziness I experienced from too much Tegretol.*

*But by Sunday I had acquired a cold due to the spread of delta in my head. The delta just got worse and my headache ever more severe as the level of Tegretol in my brain was still declining as it stabilized at 200mg. The stress of riding the Greyhound bus back to school made me very ill. I felt sick the day before school. Plus my roommates played a joke on me for April Fools Day. Carl had taken my pillow.*

*On Wednesday, April 4th I went to the Health Center to get something that might help my irritated throat. I was given a strong prescription drug that I was supposed to take three times daily. I started by taking one that afternoon around 4:30 p.m. The medicine was so strong that I decided to take it only once per day. It made me drowsy and put me to sleep.*

*The previous day, Tuesday April 3rd, I had decided to go up to 300mg on my Tegretol to help reduce delta activity in my head. By Thursday I felt like the delta was significantly reduced. I continued to take 300mg and to take the medicine prescribed to me until Sunday April 7th. I had slept in extra hours on Friday and Saturday night, so by Sunday I was feeling a lot better, I quickly tried to catch up on school work starting Sunday.*

*I watched the premiere film Twin Peaks. But I had to get up at 6:30 a.m. for a 7:00 a.m. class on Monday April 9th. I only had 7 and a half hours of sleep Sunday night. I continued to be a little short on sleep during the week, and I was stressed by this, so on Thursday night after a stressful hour watching Twin Peaks I was too stressed to sleep and I had a seizure. The seizure occurred around 1:00 a.m., two hours after I went to bed. I still made it to class at 7:00 a.m., but once I got back at 9:30 a.m. I went straight back to sleep. I had another seizure between 10:00 a.m. and 11:00 a.m. I felt so bad after that, that I did not go to my next class at noon.*

*Wednesday and Thursday night I had gone down a little on my medicine again. But the Tegretol level had nothing to do with the seizure. It was from too much stress. During Friday afternoon I recovered with sleep and I had a long recuperative sleep during the night. I felt so much better on Saturday April 14th that I went down to 200mg per day that day. I was now taking only 100mg in the morning and evening and no medicine in the middle of the day.*

*I thought that I probably would not stay on 200mg per day for as long as before. But playing racketball on Sunday with Josh and Steve helped me to increase SMR and reduce beta. I felt several periods of fuzziness from high beta while playing racketball. I even got hit in the face by the speeding racket ball (on the forehead).*

*After returning the rackets to RecSports Josh and I ran back to Mustang Village. I felt like I was breathing differently. I noticed that I was cramping in my chest, while before I had always cramped in my abdomen. The following day I noticed my butt was sore. It was sore right where I had been increasing SMR (by increasing awareness of my butt) to help me sleep. Then the next day, Tuesday April 17th, my forearms and abdomen were sore as well. Also the calves of my legs were a little sore. The interesting thing was that where I was sore corresponded to where I had to increase my awareness in order to sleep well.*

*The following days I continued to feel great on 200mg per day. From Saturday April 14th to Friday April 20th I had been on 200mg per day. I felt like a new person. On Saturday the 21st I decided I would like to go down below 200mg per day, and I started that evening.*

*More about the week of April 8th to 14th. I had gone down on my medicine all the way to 250mg per day around Monday and Tuesday. Wednesday I went back up to 300mg, but Thursday I was convinced that 300mg was too much, so I dropped back to 250mg for a couple of days to achieve an average of 280mg for the week.*

April

| Sun. | Mon. | Tues. | Wed. | Thur. | Fri. | Sat. |
|------|------|-------|------|-------|------|------|
| 8th | 9th | 10th | 11th | 12th | 13th | 14th |
| 298mg | 260mg | 250mg | 300mg | 250mg | 230mg | 200mg |

Brian's journal [April 22, 1990]

---

*I am breaking ever larger pieces of Tegretol off the 200mg pill I take each day. I take 100mg in the morning and 100mg at bedtime. At both times I break some off. I am now breaking enough off that I must be taking between 100mg and 140mg per day. I am definitely under 140mg per day. I may soon drop to 100mg per day by dividing a 200mg pill over two days.*

*I no longer feel the effects of Tegretol like before. The tension that Tegretol causes in my body is no longer felt in the chest where I felt it so much before. The last little bit of Tegretol is now manifesting itself only through tension in my forehead and face. Of course, the Tegretol has other effects, but I only notice the effect it has on my face right now. I am going down on the Tegretol because it causes me to experience a lot of high beta. I am feeling more free from the high beta that has affected me for so long.*

Brian's journal [May 6, 1990]

The particularity and detail of Brian's observations on himself continue to surprise. The fact that this continues even as the Tegretol level is reduced to this point is even more unexpected. Brian is trying to balance on the cusp of an instability.

*For the last eight days I have been taking less than 140mg of Tegretol per day. Starting Wednesday last week and continuing until Thursday this week. Wednesday night I had another epileptic seizure at about 11:45 p.m. my roommate says. I went back up to 200mg per day yesterday. Today I am feeling the consequences of raising my Tegretol. I am again experiencing lots of high beta. My arms and legs feel fuzzy here and there when I get surges of high beta.*

Brian's journal [May 11, 1990]

Brian did not have an EEG instrument at college, so his conclusions with regard to beta and delta band EEG amplitudes were based on prior associations that he had observed.

# INNER TURMOIL
## *Relationships*

*For many years I have seen people show interest in me, but I have turned it away every time. Through high school and college many pretty girls have shown interest in me, but I always turned it away. Many have felt sorry for me in the position I am with no girlfriend, and they want to help me. But I tell them, "Don't help me. There is nothing you can do, and if I did want help I could get it." If I wanted a girlfriend enough, I could have one, but I don't. I do want one, but not enough.*

*Being committed to a relationship with a woman is not something I should get myself into without some caution. My own mental and physical conditions and commitment to solving my own problems, behooves me not to make other big commitments. This is why I do not wish to get married now, but should wait a few years.*

*I have lived in isolation and misery for most of my teen years, but I value what I have been through. My experiences have taught me to value life, and friendships. Many do not care much for the friendships they develop. Many men develop relations with many women, and go through divorces. I believe I will put enough value towards a relationship with a girl that if I get married I will not divorce.*

Brian's journal [September 23, 1989]

## Progress

*What are all my efforts going to amount to? I have many ideas of where I am going, but others don't. People tell me my efforts are worthless. They definitely are not worthless, but the question still exists, where am I going in life. Where will I be when I get off the Tegretol I take and will I even get off Tegretol? Will I still be an ascetic? Will I have humor? Will head injury be revealed? Such a drastic change as overcoming epilepsy can't be all good. One does not get a gain without a loss. All along, every bit of progress I have made towards being a happier person has meant sacrificing old ways and feelings. Leaving depression is both good and bad. One becomes attached to the way he lives, even if it is miserable.*

Brian's journal [January 28, 1990]

"One becomes attached to the way he lives, even if it is miserable." The truth of this has come home to us many times during our clinical work, where the assumption that people want to get well is not always borne out. It is the whole self that needs to be comfortable with change, not just the conscious self. There is a deeper issue here. The core sense of self may be identified with the disorder. Losing the symptoms then also means losing the core self.

## Joy and Depression

> *How can I reach eternal happiness? Why am I periodically happy and depressed? Particularly, the re-occurrence of depression never ceases. I seek continuous joy. If I can eliminate all tension in my body, I eventually will be able to be eternally happy.*
>
> *Every time I am in a state of profound joy (on rare occasions) I end up going wild and the next day I feel bad again after sleeping badly. I sleep well until I reach this state of joy, after which I sleep badly.*
>
> Brian's journal [February 5, 1990]

The cyclical quality of Brian's sleep reminds me of an earlier time when Brian could sense that a seizure was impending. His brain function would deteriorate to some extent until the seizure reset things back to a starting point, and then the cycle began again. Now he may be dealing with a hypomanic state followed by descent into a depressive state that also features poor sleep.

## *More than Epilepsy*

*My epileptic problem is more than epilepsy. I can relate my problem to that of the schizophrenic syndrome. My brain is volatile. My personality fluctuates drastically. Many people conclude I am psychotic when they see me walking in a slightly somnambulant state but still conscious. I walk in a daze with little awareness of what goes on around me. Being in a sleepwalking state is having an acute awareness of a very narrow world. Most of the world you are unaware of. Thus I can focus on the road in front of me with no concept of where I am or that people are walking beside me, not even where I am going to or coming from. I program my subconscious mind to take me where I want to go without the need to be fully conscious. This is exactly like when I programmed my subconscious to get back in bed if I ever sleepwalk. Thus my body and mind is pre-programmed to do things automatically without the faculty of reason. Whenever I do not want to be present I enter this state, which often occurs as I walk around campus.*

Brian's journal [February 13, 1990]

"My epileptic problem is more than epilepsy." Indeed, Brian's condition makes a mockery of the rigid delineations of discrete diagnostic categories. His case breaches all boundaries. Of course our left-brain orientation, mine and that of the society at large, continues to rely on such categorization. There is the depression, first of all, and the hypomanic behavior that hints at a bipolar pattern. In extreme cases, we even see suicidality. There is the Aspergers-like combination of emotional blindness with logical-mathematical competence. There are the paranoid episodes. There is the episodic behavioral dyscontrol. There is the Tourette type of behavior. There are the parasomnias. And then there is the key underlying issue of an attachment problem—the inability to relate emotionally and appropriately to others. Intentions are misread, and typically biased in an adverse or hostile direction. This attachment problem was compounded out of all the others, and relates to the traumatic nature of his earlier experience. It is significant that Brian does not see the clinical categories as particularly helpful in understanding himself.

## Isolation

> *I don't want LIFE! I am a complete failure. Pursuing anything besides isolation is a mistake. I am in a despicable personality, and my doctor has kept me there, and encouraged me to go further into it, by putting me on drugs. Drugs are a limitation. But in the eyes of the public they are a liberation, and from the medical viewpoint a solution to the problem. Every action I take to gain control of my problem is seen as a selfish act by those who see it. I focus my thoughts on the actions I must take. Desire follows thought, and action follows desire. Thus think the things you know you should do and you will find yourself doing them. I have no friends, and will not*

*as long as I take this medication, thus I do not let my thoughts ever go towards thinking about girls. But other guys cannot imagine I would not think about women. Many people have tried to get me to go out with a girl, but I refuse. They conclude I am asexual or something worse.*

*I am a complete failure. My actions will all amount to nothing as long as I take drugs. Everything I do is a failure, but in other people's eyes it is a success. An action is not a success unless it is a fulfillment of what one set out to do.*

*If I set out to do something, and doing a satisfactory job is what I set out to do, then a satisfactory job is a success. But if I set out to do an excellent job, then a satisfactory job is a failure, even if the whole world thinks it is a success. Everything I have done is thus a failure. Even every class I have taken in school.*

*Isolating myself from this world is the only solution. But people do not understand that this solution could be a good thing. People think I naturally want to be with a girl. Somewhere down the road of time, I do, but not now.*

*Through isolation I will grow to understand myself and I will learn to change myself into my correct personality. Isolation is the only answer to getting out of this despicable personality. The*

*path back to a normal personality will essentially
be backwards from the path I took into it. But it
will move much faster.*

Brian's journal [February 23, 1990]

We become fully human through relationship, but sustaining relationships over the longer term depends upon a stable and reliable physiology, which Brian did not yet command. In this decision, Brian was
preceded by many generations of seekers who chose to isolate themselves to one degree or another in the service of a mental or spiritual
discipline. In Brian's case, he did not see this path as optional.

# PHILOSOPHICAL MUSINGS
## *Dualities*

*How is the mind related to the body? Separate?
Or unified as one? Can one be creative with only
logical thinking? Or is the irrational right-brain
essential to the creative process?*

*During this evening I had an interesting dis-
cussion with my roommate Josh. His friend is
trying to use both sides of his brain to achieve
higher levels of consciousness, and to improve
his concentration. His friend is ambidextrous. He
practices meditation frequently. He reads philosophy and psychology. (He would be a great
candidate for the EEG biofeedback).*

*What is God? And what does it mean to be at one with God versus to fall back on God? Some people fall back to God or Jesus to forgive them for their sins. Others search for enlightenment and unification or "oneness" with God the creator.*

*Jim says that falling back on God or Jesus to get through hard times is a lame, wimpy, way to go through life. He's a business major. One should stand up and solve his own problems. The road to freedom is making your own road, not following anyone else's. But there is more to God than depending on his love. One should not depend on God's love, but seek God with a goal in mind. A goal such as self-realization, or enlightenment.*

Brian's journal [November 17, 1989]

## The Self

*To most people there is no self separate from the personality, rather the self is the personality to many. But to me they are separate things, just as to a yogi they are as separate as oil and water.*

Brian's journal [December 9, 1989]

Brian's thinking along these lines goes all the way back to the age of eight, to the time when he had to come to terms with the misbehavior of his brain.

## Responsibility

*Is man independent or interdependent? Is one fully responsible for where he stands and who he is, and thus an independent person? Or is one only partially responsible for who he is, and everyone else also responsible?*

*A person takes more responsibility for his life than any other thing, but he does not have the power to be totally independent or responsible. Each living thing is only partially responsible for who and what he is.*

*Imagine a universe consisting of two spheres and nothing more. These two spheres can interact with one another by colliding. If two balls collide, the responsibility is in the hands of the doer and the receiver. The doer is just as responsible as the receiver.*

*If we have a universe with ten spheres, again when two collide those two are equally responsible. If one sphere collides with every other sphere, that one sphere takes a part in each of nine collisions, while every other takes a part in only one. Assuming a collision imparts a responsibility of 1 unit to both spheres involved, the distribution of responsibility for the one sphere amongst all ten looks like:*

*The sphere in the center takes 50% of the responsibility for its nine collisions. Each other sphere takes responsibility of one unit.*

*Applying this model to the real world, each person takes 50% of the responsibility for what has become of him/her, and the sum of the responsibility of all the surrounding world is also 50%. Since the sum of all things in the universe that have influence is infinite, the responsibility of a particular thing in the universe will usually be so small that it is insignificant. Since the responsibility of individual things is mostly insignificant, while the individual himself has 50% responsibility, it is often said that the individual has 100% responsibility for himself.*

Brian's journal [December 28, 1989]

## How to Change

*The intellect, emotion, and belief are all integrated together as a unit. Changing them is like molding a lump of clay. Intellect, emotion, and belief together comprise the personality, and they are masks covering the self underneath. In most people this lump of clay grows rigid at an early age. In infancy this lump of clay is soft and malleable, but stiffens up quickly. By age nine many features imprinted on this lump of clay are fixed for life. The energy required to change these features is too great, and most people would not attempt to change them. But they are not impossible to change. They can only be changed by learning how to wet the lump of clay, so that it is malleable once again. But this is a deviation from the normal progression of life. Therefore one must have a good understanding of himself or herself before he or she can suc-cessfully make a change. One must know where all the hard and soft spots are on the lump of clay, and features like cracks, punctures, protru-sions, fractures, and depressions.*

Brian's journal [February 13, 1990]

Re-molding of the clay is actually a wonderful metaphor for neuro-feedback. The active agent in that process, however, is the brain itself. It's not what Brian has in mind here, as he sees himself as the agent of change going forward.

### The Soul

*Does the spirit or soul exist in any form after death? Before birth? I believe that some spiritual entity exists before and after life as well as dur-ing. This entity exists in all life and perhaps in all things. Imagine what an insect and a human be-ing have in common, not physically, but in terms of their consciousness. This entity exists in all life, but it possesses no intellect, thought, or perception. All thought is made possible by the mind. But one can have consciousness without possessing thought.*

*Entering a state of consciousness where all thought is dispelled from the mind is the most perfect state one can be in: a "oneness" or "unity" with the world, referred to by eastern religions as "nirvana." This state of consciousness is the closest one can get to this entity; whether it is possible to reach a state equal to this entity, I do not know. I certainly have not reached that state. To reach the state of being equal with the entity is equivalent to being in perfect unity with God: In this state one has the choice at his will to live or die; his spirit could leave or enter his body. One can get close to death by going too far or too close to equality with the entity.*

Brian's journal [April 22, 1990]

## Nature of Existence

*Attempting to understand "existence" I stretch my awareness to the limit in search of integrating all sense perception together. The usual senses of sight, hearing, smell, and touch are too real to focus on alone; I look beyond these senses, seeking to be aware of all things possible. One of the most strange, misunderstood, unknown senses is our sense of consciousness. I really want to understand "existence," which leads me to study my sense of consciousness, but this is related to my awareness as a whole through all senses. As I expand my sensual awareness I lose my thinking, since my brain is limited in how much it can do at any one time. So one who attains maximum awareness through the senses also has minimized the activity of thought; but interpreting what you sense is thought; so in this state you do not interpret what is perceived.*

*This activity of trying to understand my "existence," to feel all reaches of it, leads me to interesting states of consciousness where I feel a "oneness" with the world. I feel like I have moved into perfect harmony with the universe, and that I am not separate but merged together as a unit. Imagine that the earth is part of you, and that you can perceive the existence of all life because it is part of you. If a squirrel crawls up a tree miles away, you perceive it like it's crawling up your back. This state of consciousness is the highest state of existence I can reach. I also feel like life is eternal, time does not matter, and the sensual desires of people are ridiculous and irrelevant.*

Brian's journal [May 3, 1990]

## Language

*Expression of ideas in language of whatever kind, and the process of translating from one language to another is a process that goes on inside our minds all the time. We look at the world through our senses, and applying concepts (in our knowledge and beliefs) we interpret the "raw data" that we perceive. This interpretation is one step in a translation process. As the perceptions and their interpretations are re-examined by the mind consciously and unconsciously they are modified and bear less resemblance to the actual "raw data" originally perceived. These perceptions stored in the mind become the beliefs and knowledge.*

*When speaking or writing in a language, the collection of concepts in the mind are drawn upon, and translated to the language being spoken or written. If the concepts are already stored in the language then no translation is necessary. But to limit oneself to one language is restricting. The more languages one knows the better he will be able to represent ideas. The ability to translate from one language to another is essential also, so that ideas can be related.*

*There are spoken languages, computer languages, and mathematics is another most important language. I like to relate translation in spoken languages to translation in computer languages. Beyond this, I try to think of how our thought processes in the mind could be thought of as languages.*

*The greater the bridge between the language in which we think and the language we speak the more work in translation is necessary to communicate thoughts. Realizing how large a gap exists between how I think and the English language, I am often at a loss of words to communicate my thoughts. Analogy is often my best tool for communicating my ideas.*

Brian's journal [May 5, 1990]

It is clear that thoughts may precede the language in which they are then organized and elaborated. So concept formation involves a brain process that is not strait-jacketed by language at the outset. Certainly anything emerging out of the right hemisphere starts out that way. Just as I am writing this, Sue strikes up a conversation with: "Words are really not my first language." Mental telepathy? No. Mired in a tediously long e-mail, Sue was thinking about the fact that translation is also involved when it comes to going from words back to concepts. In consequence, she does not like to engage in casual reading or casual conversation. Brian would have said the same: Words are not his first language. And I recall times when I would emerge from intense physics exams in graduate school unable to speak easily for a few hours.

What Brian here discusses in terms of mind can equally well be expressed with reference to the brain. After all, the brain cannot process sensory input directly. These inputs must be transmuted into the brain's own code. In this process they quickly become unrecognizable and untraceable. The ultimate translation challenge is what the brain manages for us easily and smoothly all the time.

## Greater Meaning

*If all I want is to be happy, and to reach the most perfect and harmonious state of existence possible, the material things are of no importance to me. Only when I dream of doing things that involve the physical world do I need material things. Life is a burden. The most enlightening experiences I have had in my life have come when I have attempted to separate spirit and body and understand the essence of existence. Death is not any worse than life. Understanding death helps one to stand fearless in the face of death and be selfless, not placing significance on material things. To reach happiness, people should stop trying to become rich, and instead try to harmonize body, mind and spirit.*

Brian's journal [May 11, 1990]

## Nirvana

*Thought involves activities outside the present, that is, when a person thinks he is interpreting what is now the past. Thought cannot exist without "raw data" to be interpreted. This "raw data" does not need to be from any particular source, but usually comes from sense perception, and does not need to be "raw" (not previously interpreted by thought). Before a person thinks, he obtains a knowledge base to think with. A knowledge base is a set of perceptions stored in some kind of memory in the brain. Awareness of thought processes inside the mind, and the ability to control them leads to the separation of body and spirit. Thought and emotion are burdens of the mind; diminished thought and emotion will lead one to the highest state of existence—nirvana. Without thought desire is nonexistent, thus nirvana frees one from all desires.*

*The less one thinks the more aware he is through sense perception (including ESP). Before a newborn baby can think he is totally involved in sense perception in the "absolute present." Once sense perception data is stored in memory the mind builds interpretation processes on this foundation of sense data.*

*As more data is collected in memory, the process of interpretation (thought) is built up and becomes more elaborate; thought processes are thus in the making. As more energy is spent thinking, less energy is spent in sense perception. As one thinks more he moves further away from the present, and eventually he learns of the concept of "time." If one does not think beyond a finite interval of time about the "absolute present," the concept of time seems nonexistent. Feelings of desire, good and bad, wrong and*

*right, importance, and a sense of time and place
all do not exist when one eliminates thought.*

*If it is possible to have no concept of time then
indeed it should also be possible to have no concept of space. But when I enter a state of timeless existence I always still have a concept of
space, though without a sense of place within
the context of space.*

Brian's journal [May 12, 1990]

Remarkably, there is indeed an entity in nature that does not experience the flow of time. It is the photon, the quantum of light. And there
may also be an entity in the universe that does not experience space. It
is consciousness itself. The capacity of one consciousness to be aware of
another seems to be independent of the distance between them.

### Dream vs. Reality

*What is the dividing line between dream and
reality? How much of life is dream and how
much corresponds to reality? The part of life
that is "dream" is comprised of images (perceptions) created entirely by the mind. That part of
life where one is conscious, and aware of what
is "real," is comprised of perceptions that are
directly related to a real world experience—that
is, the perceptions take form based on some
physical entity external to the mind/body.*

*I am aware of my level of consciousness
whether awake, asleep or half asleep. The two*

*extremes of fully conscious, and fully unconscious (asleep), are simple in nature compared to the intermediate state of semi-conscious. Sleepwalking is a semi-conscious state that I enter into purposefully during the day. Semi-consciousness involves both conscious and unconscious perceptions; dream and reality are mixed together. Although I know when I am semi-conscious, I cannot tell what corresponds to reality and what corresponds to dream when I am semi-conscious. But I am aware that this mixture of dream and reality exists.*

*When awake the senses are engaged to such a degree that one can distinguish reality and dream, but both still exist. Dream affects subconscious beliefs, and therefore the filters through which we analyze and perceive the world.*

Brian's journal [May 19, 1990]

# 6

## CAL POLY

JUNE 26, 1990 - MARCH 6, 1991

### *Software Development*

Brian spent the summer with us again, doing more programming for the neurofeedback project. He wrote a new feedback game for the Amiga called Box Lights. Three boxes of different bright colors are displayed simultaneously. Their sizes fluctuate according to the amplitude of the EEG at that moment in three spectral bands, 4-7 Hz, 12-18 Hz, and 22-30 Hz. The trainee attempts to modify the amplitudes by monitoring them continuously.

Brian had prepared the formalism for this program over the summer, and completed the game over the Christmas holidays. We also arranged for him to be paid for all of his work, so that he would have his own financial resources when he returned to college. We used the Mazes and the Box Lights program for as long as the Amiga remained commercially available in the US. Then the programs were rewritten for the PC. Both programs became so popular within the field that they were also emulated by other vendors.

Brian brought exceptional rigor to his work, as became apparent with the problems in the communications link. This thoroughness was simply a manifestation of the deliberateness with which he approached all aspects of his life. His answer to the chaos in his brain was order and regimentation in all matters—even down to managing his own facial expressions. With him, very little could be left in autopilot mode, or counted on to function unmonitored.

## Infinite

*Thought is the interpretation of the senses. Thinking takes time like a computer takes time to do calculations. Thought moves us into the past, or into the future, outside the present. As thought is dispelled from the mind, the consciousness approaches the absolute present; awareness approaches the infinite; life becomes eternal, timeless, and placeless; the body becomes fused with nature; the spirit separated from the body and selfless; all life appears to be just as much a part of the spirit as the body in which he is given a free will.*

*You cannot know how another person thinks until you can let go of your own way of thinking. To feel what another feels you need to let go of how you feel. You will only understand others to the extent that you can let go of your ways and feel what it is like to live their way.*

*You do not know what it is like to have something until you have experienced not having it as well as having it.*

*Infinite and nothing are neighbors. Approaching nothingness is approaching the infinite, and vice versa.*

*"Free will" is what makes me finite. Letting go of free will leads me to the infinite. Thought is an act of free will. Letting go of thought is my first step towards the infinite.*

*I approach the infinite, but I will always be finite. The infinite, like perfection, is something unreachable. I move closer and closer, until it seems that I am there, and I retrogress back to where I was.*

Brian's journal [June 26, 1990]


## A Deadening of the Limbs

*My successes and failures are directly related to the life and deadness of my limbs. Depression is a deadening of the limbs. Anti-convulsant drug medication is one way of making the limbs lifeless. Anti-convulsant drugs took the life out of my limbs and made my life what I have called a "complete failure." As I get off Tegretol, I am feeling revitalized. My limbs are being given life again.*

*I am down to 100mg per day on Tegretol.*

Brian's journal [June 27, 1990]

It is clear from these careful records and detailed self-observation that Brian was quite deliberate about his medication changes. His sensitivity to altering the Tegretol level is evidence for marginal brain stability.

### Heightened Awareness

*When I look at the world I apply concepts in my interpretations of it. What if I had no concepts? How then, would I interpret the world?*

*Is there knowledge without thought? Can I have knowledge about the world when I am not thinking? What form does knowledge take in my mind?*

*As thoughts are eliminated from the mind, the awareness of sense-perception is increased. This is a constant trade off that exists between thought and sense-perception. As thought mechanisms are engaged upon sensory data, the awareness of the presence of sensory data is decreased. This is a tradeoff between two different mental activities. I wish to inquire further into the nature of the less familiar of these mental activities, namely sense-perception and awareness.*

*When the mind is focused on the absolute present, and thought is eliminated, the mind/ body reaches a state of heightened awareness. My mind seems to have a heightened knowledge of some form when so aware. But I hold no concepts about the world, not even of the existence of space or time. I hold only one concept that beneath all others I have been unable to eliminate: the concept that I exist, although I do not know in what form I exist, or that there is any form to existence at all. Form is a concept, so I do not think of this concept when I have eliminated all my thoughts.*

*In this heightened awareness I see so much, but perceive nothing, interpret nothing. If I interpreted the world I would be thinking. I feel like I have this infinite knowledge (or approach it) when I reach heightened awareness. Yet when I have this heightened awareness the knowledge is lost or becomes inexplicable with the limitation of language. What is the form of this knowledge, and the nature of it in my mind? Does there exist a language to describe it?*

Brian's journal [June 28, 1990]

The brain has an immense store of "implicit knowledge" about its environment, all of which is encoded non-verbally. This implicit knowledge establishes our real identity, our relationship to the outside world, and thus our sense of safety in the world. It is possible that in this state

of heightened awareness Brian is encountering this realm of implicit
knowledge through feeling states. This domain can only be apprehend-
ed. It defies articulation.

> *I felt so good yesterday evening that I went to
> bed without taking any medicine. I have been
> taking about 60mg per day the last five days, and
> for two weeks I have been under 100mg per day.
> Last night I dropped to zero milligrams. I do not
> know whether I will be able to repeat this tonight,
> but I expect to. I have never before dropped to
> zero milligrams in a night successfully. When I
> felt great and didn't want to take any Tegretol, by
> about two or three a.m. I became very suscepti-
> ble to a seizure.*
>
> Brian's journal [July 13, 1990]

This report demonstrates the fast-acting nature of Tegretol, which
makes all this fine-tuning possible. I can only imagine how a neurologist reading this might react. I would not be surprised if this kind of
report is unprecedented in their entire medical experience.

## A Cry for Help

> *A crying voice I heard. "Something is in agony;
> someone is in pain," I thought as this cry woke
> me from my half asleep state. A few voices from
> the other bedrooms responded, and soon some-
> one opened my door slightly to see if I was okay.
> I made a remark, upset about all this uproar. But
> most vivid in my mind was this recognition that*

*something—although I did not know what—was in agony. This thing in agony: dog, cat, human, or beast. I did not know what species it was.*

*By the nature or tone of the message I felt the animal must have intelligence. Either it was a very intelligent animal, or it was a human. But most vivid in what I saw, was the injury of a limb—one used to hold the weight of the body. So if the animal was human it must be the human leg, not an arm, or if the animal is a dog or cat it could be any of four limbs. Yet the feeling remained that the limb was a hind leg, NOT a foreleg. Since dogs are bare-foot, but humans usually wear shoes it seemed more reasonable that the animal was a four-legged animal, like dog or cat. I concluded that the animal is probably not human. Yet the animal had an amazingly high level of intelligence, and possessed a strength and body mass comparable to myself.*

*So is this animal a wild cat (mountain lion) or a bear? Such an animal could possess the intelligence and strength I recognize this animal to have.*

*There was still an uproar in the house. Something was going on. I felt that whatever this animal was, it was now being helped by those who had gotten up out of bed. So I tried to calmly go back to sleep. I continued to wonder if Chaco or Rontu (my two dogs) had been injured.*

*Soon all was quiet, and I thought they were probably on the way to the hospital with Chaco.*

*It later occurred to me that I had never heard Siegfried's voice, but had heard Kurt's and Sue's voice. I briefly felt that Siegfried might be hurt, and might be the one in agony. I dismissed the thought that Siegfried was the one in agony, and decided that he was probably a little bit hurt from trying to help an injured animal. I still believed that the crying in agony was from a dog or cat.*

*Much later, after everyone was back from the trip to the hospital or wherever they went, I felt a slight pain of something severing my foot. I felt as if something sharp had cut the tender part on the bottom of my foot, in the crease between the ball of the foot. Since Siegfried had talked about swimming last night, and (my uncle) Hans was asking questions about the Sierra Nevada (over the phone), I dreamt of a lake or stream in the Sierra Nevada, and I was walking barefoot into the stream. I was stepping on sharp rocks, and was almost cutting myself on them.*

*After this long sleep last night I woke up rather sleepy this morning, as if from a troubled sleep.*

*The trouble that my parents had sleeping last night, I had also felt.*

*I had never supposed Siegfried was the injured one who cried out last night. Everything seemed rather strange with Sue sleeping in the living room when I got up this morning. Discovering this morning that Siegfried had injured his foot surprised me, and led me to write this recollection of what I experienced.*

*The whole event occurred on the night of July 2nd, Monday. I was impressed by what association existed between what I sensed and what actually happened. This story is a recollection of what may be partially a telepathic experience.*

Brian's journal [July 3, 1990]

The message I was sending (yelling!) was that I needed help. On the night of July 2, I was working late on my home computer. At the end of the day, after midnight, I decided to take the garbage out as a last item before heading to bed. My thoughts clearly were elsewhere. I was barefoot. I did not even bother to turn on the light in the kitchen. I took the grocery bag out of the container, rather than taking the whole container. It held a heavy glass jar, which fell out of the bottom of the bag, and shattered on the floor. I attempted to step over the shards, but instead stepped right onto one of them, and lacerated my foot. I yelled for Sue at the other end of the house. It was a long distance from the back door all the way to the bedroom and it was difficult to be heard from one end of the house to the other. Eventually, Sue heard me and came to my aid in the kitchen.

It is interesting to see how this event intruded upon Brian's awareness in his quasi-sleep state, and how the mind immediately structures
a context that makes sense out of the intruding information.

On a side note, after I was stitched up in the emergency room at Encino Hospital the wound became infected over the course of the following several days. It was the July 4th holiday. "This is an angry wound,"
said my family doctor when we finally got to see him. The foot had to
be opened up again and cleaned out. I spent three days on antibiotic
drip at Sherman Oaks Hospital, all the while soberly reflecting on Jim
Henson of Muppets fame, who had just succumbed to an unmanageable infection a few months earlier. This was a very close call.

## Seizures

*Both Saturday and Sunday night I had one or
more seizures from allspice in my father's birthday cake. Last night was my first night of recovery. I am down to 30mg per day on Tegretol.*

*If I continue to try to go down I will be off
before I go back to school.*

*Today, after one night without an epileptic sei-
zure, my abdomen is sore from the way I am
now breathing. When I have seizures I breathe
mostly in my chest, but now I am breathing more
uniformly over my whole body. When resting,
breathing should feel like inflating a balloon. The
pressure inside the balloon is the same everywhere over the inside surface. With all parts of
my body relaxed I should feel the pressure inflating me at all points around my body. Thus*

*when I inhale, my fingers and toes feel like they are being inflated, and in proportion with my arms and legs being inflated. Feeling equal inflation of every part of my body means that oxygen is being distributed evenly around my body. When one part of me feels like it is not being inflated, I know if is not getting an equal share of oxygen. Also, if I give too much oxygen to some part of me, then it is misused and work is done wastefully.*

Brian's journal [July 23, 1990]

Regrettably, it took a second night of seizure activity before Sue rushed to check the birthday cake for ingredients. Sure enough, there was allspice in the cake. The low dose of Tegretol was yielding Brian very little buffer against dietary insults. While Brian was mentally on a path of getting off the medication, I remember being acutely concerned about him at this time. His EEG was worse than I had ever seen it before. It was often dominated by very low frequency (delta) activity, manifesting considerable lack of control and instability.

We thought it high time to visit a neurologist, which we had not done since our off-putting experience with Dr. Menkes, and we convinced Brian that this was a good idea. On the advice of Brenda Comings, we made an appointment to see Dr. David Comings, with whom we already had a good relationship, at the City of Hope. "He already knows Brian so well," she said. We were working with Dr. Comings at that time on a joint research project on Tourette Syndrome that was testing the effects of Clonidine and the effects of neurofeedback. Comings was an expert on brain/behavior relationships.

We had an extended appointment in which Dr. Comings reviewed Brian's medical history in detail. In the manner of a traditional family doctor, he talked to Brian at length. Brian did not really want to be there, and showed his annoyance. Comings pointed out to him that at times he was near losing emotional control; that everyone there was being exceedingly careful in talking with him. Brian listened. This was a different doc. He was actually paying attention to Brian, and interested in him. Comings was gaining his trust.

Dr. Comings suggested a trial of Prozac. A prescription of Dilantin was also provided that Brian could use to complement the Tegretol if he felt that he needed it. Brian was unwilling to admit the possibility that he may have to go back on Dilantin. That battle had been won so long ago that he did not want that question reopened. However, he was willing to allow for the possibility. Dr. Comings told us that it was quite common for young adults in their early twenties to abandon their medication. It was particularly a problem among those with bipolar disorder, who would give up their lithium, but also among those with seizure disorders.

Brian tried the Prozac for a period of time. He took only 2.5mg per day, much less than the standard minimum dose, yet it had a profound effect on him. He sometimes exhibited episodes of manic behavior, states of unusual euphoria and high activity level, which we assumed was caused by the Prozac, although his dosage was very small. We also witnessed times of spaciness, and the lack of his usual mental acuity, as on the three days he took off from his computer work. The Prozac was abandoned.

We also took Brian back to Dr. Marshall for some shots. Brian had not seen him for years. It was business as usual, like the old days when Sue was a regular visitor with one or another child. Before we had gotten back into the treatment room, or even had a chance to tell Marshall why we were there, he had already barked orders to his staff for all sorts of blood tests, etc., amounting to hundreds of dollars. I wanted to object, but the opportunity hardly presented itself.

Why were we doing blood levels on Tegretol? It would have zero influence on what level Brian was taking. Why were we testing for liver toxicity after Brian had taken the medication for umpteen years already? It seemed to be defensive medicine at its worst.

When we met with Dr. Marshall, Brian started to tell him of his progress in reducing the medication. Marshall cut him off. "Brian, you are going to be on this medication for the rest of your life. Face it. Don't play games." I had been hoping to get Marshall to persuade Brian to consider trying Dilantin again, or perhaps some other anticonvulsant. But this was not going well. He was talking to Brian as if he were still eight years old. He was a pediatrician, after all. He could not shift gears to talk to a 21-year-old. As he talked, I could see the hair standing up on Brian's neck, figuratively speaking. He would prove Marshall wrong! Marshall had not taken the time to acknowledge Brian's progress. He was not interested to know who Brian was now. As far as Brian was concerned, Marshall did not yet have talking rights.

We left the office worse off than when we came in, financially and in all other ways. We never went back. This was standard medicine at its worst. People are not the sum total of their lab test results. We assume that the lab results held no surprises. We never called to find out.

Brian's EEG continued to show large-amplitude low-frequency activity, and normalized only slowly after the two seizures. We were very concerned. And we still had not seen a neurologist.

*The month of August has begun. Summer seems to be passing quickly. I have been going down on the Tegretol I take. I also had a few seizures while I tried to live on no Tegretol. I am now back on 30mg per day. Rather than going lower at this time, I am focusing my efforts on improving the states of consciousness in which I spend my waking and sleeping hours. Being low on Tegretol has made me spacey. Exercise, stretching, meditation, and other kinds of men-*

*tal focus all help me to improve control over my states of consciousness. I have taken the last three days away from my computer to improve my state of consciousness. Today I am very sore from all the time I have spent in a full lotus posture. My body has become "loose" from sitting in the lotus posture.*

*Too much time in front of my computer is damaging psychologically. I need to balance time in front of my computer with time to exercise and socialize.*

*I am well below the therapeutic range of Tegretol. As I have moved to lower levels of Tegretol the effect that I feel from the Tegretol changes. Especially, the location of this most intense effect has continued to shift. Originally the effect of the Tegretol was felt mostly in the frontal area of my brain. As I moved down to levels of 200mg per day the effect was no longer most intense in my forehead but had shifted back to mid-brain. Now the area where the Tegretol is felt is in the brainstem. I am now on 30mg per day. As my whole brain becomes a working unit I will become normal again.*

Brian's journal [August 3, 1990]

*Moving to lower levels of Tegretol by relatively large increments, cutting dosage to one-third for example: the most difficult change that has been necessary was letting go of tension in my chest and forehead resulting in an associated change in the way I breathe. As the way I breathe changes, I experience changes psychologically. My psychological state could be associated with the way I breathe, probably in a one-to-one relationship.*

*Letting go of tension has resulted in the freeing of many emotions that for most of my life have been unfelt (non-existent). At first it seemed as if all of a sudden so much responsibility was unleashed that I could not deal with it. The way I dealt with this new freedom was to relax. Above all else, I needed to relax. Let my sensory cortex of my brain be free and not fixed under tension.*

*Letting go of tension in the forehead and chest has been fundamental to getting down to lower levels of Tegretol. But this tension also seems to be fundamental to surviving and coping with Tegretol. I have just gone up on my level of Tegretol again. I have made my way to very reduced levels of tension, but now that I triple my dosage today, moving from 30mg to 100mg per day, I experience dizziness and drowsiness. I feel ill. I also recognize that by increasing the tension in*

*my forehead I easily reduce all feelings of dizzi-*
*ness, drowsiness, and illness.*

Brian's journal [August 6, 1990]

Brian had discovered the power over our own physiology that we possess by virtue of our control of the breath. When it comes to modulating our nervous system level of activation, our strongest tool is through manipulation of the breath. Just decreasing the breathing rate shifts us toward parasympathetic dominance and greater calmness. Usually, this is also stabilizing.

Brian's reference to his forehead brings to mind that at this point we were still some years away from knowing how to train the pre-frontal region of cortex. This might have been very helpful to Brian. Partly that delay was a consequence of our success. The results we were getting drove us to refine our methods rather than looking for more cortical terrain to conquer. There was a rationale for doing this kind of training on the motor strip of cortex, and so we were tethered to that placement for a long time.

### Strict Discipline

*People develop functions performed in the brain*
*stem long before they have well developed func-*
*tions in the forebrain. That is to say, motor activa-*
*tion and deactivation—sleeping and waking—are*
*skills generally learned before skills of reason,*
*like solving math problems. Skills of reason I*
*have always felt were in the front of my brain.*
*Therefore, when anticonvulsant drugs limited my*
*abilities mentally and physically, I counteracted*
*the drugs with effort to make my mental skills*
*as good as I possibly could. It was a trade-off,*

*deciding what part of my brain I would control and what part Tegretol and Dilantin would control.*

*I gave up the ability to have free will over a large part of the way I felt every day. I chose to be fixed and unchanging in many aspects of my psychology. I accepted that I would probably never be happy and never have friends; I accepted "strict discipline" as the only way I could ever bring any feeling of respect into my life. Since I have almost no control of myself, I accept good effort on my part as the only excuse I can give to living this way. Either I work as hard as I can to discipline myself, or I die. Strict discipline and hard work has brought me self-respect, and this is the only kind of self-respect I have since I am a complete failure in all respects. The only thing that makes me worth anything is the fact that I work hard. But the work I have done deserves little respect since it is mostly failures.*

Brian's journal [August 7, 1990]

How is one to understand this from someone who stands at or near the top of his class in computer science and in math? How is one to understand this from a guy who surely exercises more personal discipline in more dimensions of existence than anyone else he knows? These ideas simply do make sense in a rational frame. Brian's emotional maelstrom ever intrudes into his struggle toward ordered thought.

## *Angry Expressions*

*I expect the world to be tough, and hard work. My father always looks at me with an angry expression, or at least never with a happy one. He may look at others with a happy face. I see him smile in conversations with other people, but he never smiles at me.*

*I look at my father with an angry expression, and he looks at me with an angry expression. We hardly ever communicate. If there is any communication between us, it always seems to be a correction to my behavior: "Don't do that." He tells me how to act in many respects, but he never tells me how I should feel. I have always seemed to make him content by being passive. When I act he is always upset with how I act. Especially he is always upset by me playing with my brother. If I try to have fun with my brother, my father is mad at me and punishes me or simply separates us. Since there is never a time when my father encourages me to play with my brother, and he never encourages any communication between me and any family member, I get the picture that I am expected to be silent, and to never say a word unless absolutely necessary. I should never interact with my brother. All play is discouraged.*

*I am generally silent and hold an angry
mood. Feeling miserable, in pain, and like life
is very difficult is how I should feel, I think. If I
am hyperventilating, feeling extremely worked,
experiencing pain and suffering, then everyone
is happy.Everyone will be most happy if I am
in great torment, because torment goes along
with punishment.*

Brian's journal [August 11, 1990]

Ouch! Brian is clearly undergoing another very difficult period. But the asymmetry in our relationship, that I was more riveted on the negatives than the positives in his life, may well be true. I was working out of the home, and so I needed to remain engaged with my work unless my intervention was called for. That's a formula for the asymmetry of which Brian complained. As long as things were going well around the house, I was not there for him. Worried about his ongoing seizures, I was surely looking at Brian with profound concern and sadness, which he interpreted as disapproval. There was silence, too, the silence of biting my tongue to let him be who he wanted to be.

Brian's lament with regard to being punished for trying to "have fun" with his brother is a recapitulation of his entire life with Kurt rather than a reflection of the state of affairs at the time of writing. In earlier days it would indeed be only a matter of time before Kurt would seek out one or both of us in order to be rescued from his big brother. So we were always on guard when they were playing together. At this time, there wasn't much occasion for play in that relationship. Kurt recalls that by this point he was having interesting two-way conversations with Brian, as opposed to just being lectured to, as had been the case earlier.

*For the last two days Kurt and I have been alone
in the house without Sue or Siegfried around,*

*and what a relief it has been. I have been kept busy in front of my computer developing software. When other family members are under a lot of pressure, it is hard not to feel a little of it too.*

Brian's journal [August 11, 1990]

We were presenting our first course on EEG training for health professionals. It took place at our San Francisco office. I was still on crutches after the foot injury. Dr. Michael Linden attended this first training course. He has since become an authority on neurofeedback for ADHD. And Dr. David Comings came with his wife Brenda. He was becoming recognized as an authority on Tourette Syndrome. We only had a dozen or so professionals at our first course, but this launched us nicely into a new direction in our work. It had become clear to me that mental health providers would hear about this revolutionary new method far more readily from colleagues than from outsiders, so we wanted to build a large practitioner community as quickly as possible.

### Kurt

*With all this pressure from my parents, being around my brother is often the best way to get a little relief. When Kurt is not under pressure to do work, we get along o.k. While when Kurt is doing work for my father, or practicing his piano music, I go off and sit alone somewhere.*

*Recently I had seizures from trying to cope with too low a dosage of Tegretol. I have moved back up to 100mg per day, from only 30mg per day. Because I did not entirely cope with only 30mg per day, I felt a stronger presence of my father looking at me like I am some angry beast with evil intentions. My mother sometimes looks at me like I am selfish and inconsiderate, and even has told me so.*

*Kurt has been eager to be in charge of cooking. Feeling the relief of not having my parents around me all the time, I have been in the mood to relax. I have let Kurt do all the cooking, and I have been enjoying myself.*

*Kurt has kept the pool in good condition for swimming, and we fixed the hole in the fence that the dogs escaped through to get out of the yard.*

*Yesterday, Kurt and I went to see Air America. Today Kurt, Chris, and I went to see Problem Child, which is the funniest movie I have ever seen. Never has a movie kept me laughing so much from one moment to the next.*

*Life seems so relaxed and "carefree" without my parents around. Even though I am doing laundry, cleaning the house, and cleaning dishes, preparing food, I still feel so much more secure and comfortable with Kurt around, and the television to watch. I am more secure than at school because I don't have a roommate who enjoys creating trouble, and there is not the noise of neighbors blasting music.*

Brian's journal [August 11, 1990]

Kurt was the more emotionally mature of the two, despite being seven years younger, and given the situation, Kurt no doubt made Brian his priority over those days of our absence. Keeping Brian happy was the key to his own well-being during this time. All their years together had been tough on Kurt. He lived literally in fear of physical abuse at the hands of his irascible brother for a number of years, to a degree that we were not fully aware of. Picked on at school, Brian no doubt took it out on his little brother whenever the two were alone. Kurt, in turn, developed survival skills in handling bullies. He learned to parry Brian's malign intentions by various means of distraction and misdirection. This is also how Dick Gregory first got into comedy. He developed his comedic skills as a way of keeping from getting beaten up. Kurt likewise was a born entertainer with great verbal agility.

Kurt later told us that his greatest vulnerability was at times when Sue demurred from serving as referee of their altercations. "You sort it out," she might say in final capitulation. This was Kurt's worst fear, as that left him completely at Brian's mercy.

With Brian now 21 years old, this prior history was long in the past, and Brian had begun to appreciate his brother. Kurt, on the other hand, was primed for the challenge of managing his still unpredictable brother on the basis of long years of experience.

## SCHOOL LIFE
### *Wild Swings*

> *I feel ready to go back to school this Friday and I feel like a very different person than I was one year ago, and different than I was two months ago. My brain waves have been taking wild swings this summer with my efforts to get off*

*Tegretol. Although my EEG was quite wild with a threshold of 30 microvolts on the theta inhibit, I was moving toward a new way of using my brain, which has now stabilized and made me quite a different person at least from my perspective, but perhaps not from others'.*

*One year ago I was starting a wild school year, in which I experimented with lowering the Tegretol I take. I never liked Tegretol. Tegretol brings depression with agitation into my life, and it makes my mind foggy. I went from 600mg per day to 200mg per day during the nine months of school. Going this route changed my life drastically, but changes were limited to clearer thought during the day and better sleep—but not much else. There was little change to my emotional life.*

*This summer I tackled the emotional problems that still lingered. I realized the need to expand how much of my brain I use, and to decrease the intensity with which I use the front of my brain. Like a spring with a weight, oscillating up and down, I oscillated up and down about the equilibrium point in my brain. The more drastically my EEG went to "high," the more drastically low it went: that is, the variation of my EEG in each area of my brain tended to average out to the same equilibrium values, regardless of the*

*magnitude of the excursions. But I did not want
a wide range of variation in my EEG.*

Brian's journal [September 11, 1990]

Stability of function is the overriding issue at this point, and Brian saw this clearly as going far beyond the issue of seizures. His level of function varied dramatically with the state of his brain, and this affected everything—his cognitive functioning, his emotions, motor control, and the quality of sleep. One could even see this in the quality of handwriting in his journal, which fluctuated in a manner that correlated with his functional status.

Over time, this emphasis on brain stability also came to dominate our own thinking with regard to neurofeedback strategies. It is an issue that crosses diagnostic boundaries. This shifts the perspective to the brain functioning as our control system, as it is the primary burden of any self-regulating control system to maintain its own stability.

## New Roommates

*This first week of Fall Quarter has been quite
eventful. Settling into a new apartment with new
roommates; enduring two nights with paprika in
my system, and meeting a counselor at Student
Services to talk about developing social skills.*

*My first two nights at this apartment, I had
breathing episodes in my sleep because of the
level of stress associated with adjusting to a
new place. On the third night I ate some of the
taco salad J. made, but the salad had paprika
in it and I asked too late. I was able to focus
so that I slept with no seizure that night, but the*

*next night I had some rough breathing episodes. Forty-eight hours after eating the taco salad the paprika was out of my system enough so that I slept well again.*

*Continued practice of Yoga exercises I learned is helping me sleep better and improving my life. The "chest expansion" has been the most helpful in improving my sleep, and the complete breath, either standing or sitting helps me sleep better.*

*As my breath is gradually becoming more complete, I am gradually feeling more full of life. Relaxation is becoming a way of life.*

Brian's journal [September 22, 1990]


### *Re-adjusting*

*Last week was so long because I was re-adjusting to school life. I visited several different offices and people finding out what is available to me so that I can make the best of all that is offered here. I have applied to a math honor society here (KME), and I am looking around at other groups I might join, like the "Amiga User's Group." I have also spoken with another counselor this week, and I am joining the social skills group. The social skills group focuses on developing self-esteem and increasing trust and capacity to care for others. I meet this afternoon at 3:00 p.m. with this group.*

*Today I saw a friend from a math class, Andrew, who is President of KME, I think. Andrew said he has been looking for me and couldn't remember my name. He said he would like me to join KME, and I told him that I have applied.*

*I may apply to get a minor in math. I want to take more math simply out of interest, and a math minor looks like a relatively simple thing to get.*

Brian's journal, [September 27, 1990]

## *Yoga*

*Besides all the groups I am looking at, and all my organizations, I am doing yoga on a regular basis every day. Yoga is having a profound effect on how I feel every day and night. My sleep is significantly improving. I am continuing to move gradually towards a complete "unification" of all aspects of my inner self. As my breath becomes more balanced or "even throughout" I am experiencing more of life. I was once half-living because I was half-breathing. Now I am breathing fully. I sleep deeper by breathing more fully.*

*Yoga will continue to be a practice every day for me. The benefits I am experiencing from*

*yoga have not stopped or slowed down. Yoga continues to bring new benefits every day.*
Brian's journal [September 27, 1990]

## Jujitsu

*Tonight I went for the second time to a group practicing Jujitsu. I feel like my focus has improved. Mental focus and feeling energy channels through my arms and legs is essential to completing a throw. In every movement I start by feeling the energy channel through my arms (spreading fingers), and then I make a movement while maintaining balance that knocks my opponent off balance. Throughout the movements I hold my opponent under tension—that is, I have him in a lock that may be painful. While holding this tension I continue to move in a graceful, balanced, and un-tensed manner; force is not applied with muscular exertion. All moves are done in an effortless manner.*

*The benefits I have experienced are: release of tension, better mental focus or concentration. The way one moves without using muscular force and with a special focus requires that you be relaxed. Feeling energy channels is being relaxed. The special focus necessary here is part*

*of what differentiates the benefit I am getting
from Jujitsu versus that of yoga.*

Brian's journal [October 5, 1990]


## Socialization

*This week has been full of meaningful events,
and has been the most stressful week yet this
quarter because of midterms. Both Wednesday and Thursday night I experienced seizures
of some form, but Friday night after practicing
Jujitsu I slept very well—not only without
seizure, but deeply rested and refreshed.*

*I am slowly moving out of my long deep period
of being "phased-out" by the drugs I have taken
for epilepsy. Soon I will be free of seizures and
the medication taken for epilepsy. For so long
any attempt to develop a relationship, or any
kind of friendship of significance, was meaning-
less since I was so displeased with my own way
of life. I recognized that I must be happy with
myself before I can make friends. Often though,
I have been full of pride and some happiness, so
I was puzzled about why I continued to fail. The
anticonvulsant drugs I took kept me feeling low,
and without emotion or humor. I was even considered to be ASEXUAL by some of my peers,
and I did feel totally devoid of any sexual drive.*

*As all aspects of my life are improving, so too must the social aspect. I am feeling a need to socialize and have friends.*

*I have just watched the movie* Clockwork Orange, *and I am thinking about why I choose to be alive and not dead. Why not die and pass into perfection? With no body, the spirit by itself is perfect.*

Brian's journal, [October 13, 1990]

Many years earlier, shortly after the movie Clockwork Orange was released, we were playing the sound track at home. Brian told us to turn it off. The disturbing theme of the movie was very well embodied in the music, and Brian found it very unsettling.

## Emotional Growth

*The last three months could be called a period of emotional growth, but it has been much more than just emotional growth. Every day the subconscious imbalances would fluctuate—approaching and regressing from a more balanced state. As I achieved a better balance of emotions, I also noticed a regression back to a less balanced state, like a fire burning my heart and frying my brain. Emotions would be poured out like never before. My feelings became pillars in the sense that they are a new foundation from which I build "life experience." I have often wished that in the context of being around people I'd have no emotions. I have succeeded in concealing all emotion and being analytical. Although I could restrict my emotion well, it would always be there.*

Brian's journal [December 9, 1990]

Emotion in the singular. Brian is concerned with the quantity—its intensity—here more than its character. The language is about balance, but the core issue is containment of the excesses, the burning of the heart and the frying of the brain.

## Christmas Vacation

*What shall I do for these four weeks of vacation over Christmas? Today is Sunday, December 9, 1990. Fall Quarter 1990 ended Friday December 7th, when I had my last final. Fall Quarter has been a period of constant change for me, and I am not sure how to describe this change. I am now home in Sherman Oaks, and at a loss for "things to do."*

Brian's journal [December 9, 1990]

## Against Suicide

*In interpersonal group this week we discussed the relationships people had with their parents. I had described my feelings of inferiority and worthlessness that I experienced in childhood and early in college, and I said what also gave my life the little "worth" that it had. The idea of being "worthless" brought up the topic of depression and suicide. We discussed rebellion from family, and temptation (if any) for suicide. But suicide does not relate to me (I think), because it is against my values.*

Brian's journal [February 5, 1991]

There had been times, of course, when death seemed benign, if not welcome. At those times, suicide would have appeared to be a sensible option.

## Tension

*Yesterday ended with some tension introduced as I spoke to Sue over the phone. I kept myself up a few minutes too long (11:15 p.m.), and released tension by some jerking about. My sleep was a little rough but adequate. I had a slight headache that permeated my entire head as I perceived it. The lack of a focus point of pain, and the even distribution throughout is a good indication of improvement in how I respond to body tension.*

*This week started out like a peaceful week. I had improved my level of relaxation and "opening up" to people I see during the day. More happy/ casual interchanging of words with people. Yet I still feel more subtle tensions present. Occasional impulses of tension still occur.*

Brian's journal [February 8, 1991]

So much of Brian's concern wraps around the quality of sleep. He knew that it was key to his level of functioning the following day, and he knew that he could influence the kind of sleep that he would likely get the following night. This turns out to be a far more general truth, but most clinicians don't have an opportunity to observe the sleep of their clients. One who did so, a learning disabilities specialist I had met in 1989 in San Diego, found that every one of her child clients exhibited anomalies in their sleeping EEG. This does not tell us, however, whether it reflects correlation or causation.

## PHILOSOPHICAL MUSINGS
### The Role of Mathematics in Nature

*There exists some language that describes how nature works; and a set of laws in that language. The language is mathematics, and the laws are the laws of physics. At one time I wanted to study physics because I want to know how the world works, but I decided math is what I should study because to develop new theories about how nature works I need to know nature's language—mathematics. As mathematics creates new fields of study, physics will soon follow up with applications of the new field of mathematics. As this process continues, some day there will be a physical explanation for phenomena like telepathy. Some day we will know the effect one's thoughts can have on the people around him. The world is far more complex than people realize. All our concepts about the world are only approximations of the true way the world is. We construct models of the world, and all models have limitations.*

*We may never know the essence of consciousness, and physical explanations of strange psychological phenomena like telepathy. But physical explanations of these phenomena do indeed exist. Before we will have answers to these phenomena, mathematics, the science of complexity, and other natural sciences must be further unified. Many disparate fields of science need to be recognized for their unseen association or similarities. Mathematics will bring us closer to describing nature when new advances are made in computer simulations—what might also be called "the science of complexity."*

Brian's journal [September 23, 1990]

Indeed we may never come to know the essence of consciousness scientifically. What Brian is coming to realize is that science deals with descriptions rather than essences. We never get to the essence of things in science. Paradoxically, Brian is closest to the essence of consciousness in his experience of it.

### Accomplishment

*Since birth I felt the need to have a reason for every act that is in my free will—including life itself. Why do I live? If I am going to take on life I must have a purpose or goal, otherwise life is pointless and should be terminated. Life is hard work, so if I am going to live I need to have some reward or sense of accomplishment in life. "Sense of accomplishment" is purely the one most important—and possibly only—good feeling that gives me a reason to live. "Accomplishment of what?" you might ask. Observing that I have a mind and body I seek to understand it and the world that surrounds me. I want to know what life is. My sense of accomplishments comes from achievement of goals I set out to achievo.*

*Since I have been so goal-oriented since birth, I also have regarded "accomplishment," the pride that follows it, to be the only pleasure in life. Life is not pleasure, but pain and suffering. I must be self-sufficient from birth to death. Life is full of hard work, but it brings reward. Thus I live as others would like me to, and not as I would like to. I believed that I would not enjoy life.*

Brian's journal [October 13, 1990]


**Non-attachment**

*If I were to associate a word with this week's emotion, then it would be "non-attachment."*

*Non-attachment to all actions, emotions, and thoughts. Tests went by, but no stress ever occurred; I left each exam feeling calm, and content, as if I had been having fun. I occasionally say "hello" or "hi" impulsively to people, and this reflects a kind of attachment to feelings. Non-attachment to all emotions at all times is desirable. Whether in pleasure or pain, be content.*

Brian's journal [February 5, 1991]

Brian was taking a course in Eastern religions.

## FINAL ENTRIES
### *A Hindu Temple*

*Today I had an experience I shall never forget: visiting a Hindu temple, worshipping Siva and Vishnu. In a gathering before a temple dedicated to Siva, people chanted to the beat of drums and strumming of a string instrument.*

*Many aromas (smells) were floating about and the smoke from a fire. Opening my right hand, a sacred offering of an opaque milk white liquid was given, and I sipped a little, pouring the majority of it on my head.*

*Standing before deities like Ganesh or Siva, I felt an energy field. Ganesh was a purifying/ cleansing feeling. Vishnu was warmth/love. The former was cool, while the latter was warm. The cool or warm feeling was a good feeling in both cases.*

*During the entire visit I had my shoes and socks off. All offers were accepted with the right hand. The left hand is the "toilet paper hand" in India.*

*The priest would, at appropriate times, walk by with flame. I would put my hands up to the flame to feel the warmth, and bring my hands up to my face so my face could feel tho warmth.*

*Sacred offerings of fruits—banana, pears, coconut, and nuts & raisins—were given following praying in front on Siva and feeling the flame. I received a banana, piece of coconut, and a few nuts. The fruit is to be eaten, and must not be thrown away.*

*After attending a short worship of Vishnu, we went to eat lunch in the temple. A mild food consisting of yogurt and rice mixed with a little flavor was served, along with a little spicy food that could be mixed with the mild food. The spicy food was the spiciest I had ever eaten in my life, much spicier then the spiciest Mexican food I have ever eaten.*

*After lunch I met someone outside who appeared to be a spiritual man of great stature, although he appeared young—in his twenties, I think. He considers himself to be a Yogi, and he had some interesting advice. He recommended that I read Maharishi Mahesh Yogi's translation of the Gita. To learn more about herbs and cooking, philosophy, and anything to do with Yoga, he mentioned the Bodhi Tree Bookstore in West Hollywood. "Gotu Kola" (Brahmi in Sanskrit) is an herb that calms the mind, and it can be used in tea—typically 1/2 a teaspoon.*

Brian's journal [February 17, 1991]

## Clarity of Mind

*I woke up this morning at 7:40 a.m., I was up and dressed by 8:00 a.m. I felt so fresh and clear, so "awake" that I thought the fact I was just sleeping seemed impossible or just odd. To what extent is this clarity of mind due to the tea I drank last night with Gotu Kola? Because I ate a bowl of cereal before drinking tea, I thought the effect of the Gotu Kola would be diluted. Apparently the Gotu Kola still has an effect later on in the night, as my friend had said "It will not take effect immediately, and the following morning you will feel a profound peace of mind." My experience is just what my friend had said it would be. But a sleep so deep and cleansing of all stress is a common occurrence the night following a morning when I get up early—like 5:00 a.m. or 6:00 a.m. Thus other factors are playing a part in this. The food I ate is another factor. I believe that I sense an effect (positive) that is exclusively from the tea. Even if I had slept deeply without the tea, I would not have reached the profound peace of mind I felt today.*

Brian's journal [February 18, 1991]

## Letting Go

*Some weeks aro peaceful, others not. "Unpeaceful" best describes my feelings this week. While last week was relaxed, this week seemed every day was full of havoc. Not external havoc, but internal. Every moment I felt stressed and unhappy. Although many of my activities—social and academic—are all going well, something inside me was psychologically not right. Somehow I had too many things to do, and not enough time to get to know myself. I must keep in touch with my needs—food, water, breath, and heart (emotion); but not think too intensely. By thinking too much, a seizure was inevitable Wednesday night—necessary to release mental tension.*

*Thursday afternoon was my first attempt to remedy this unpeaceful "self." Since the havoc was internal, not manifested externally, I was uncertain how to explain it. Describing my "troubled" self, I was helped by the words of people who listened to my words and feelings.*

*Today I have attempted to further "let go" and to "live in the present." "To hell with my Linear Algebra," I need to live and breathe this very present moment. Stop living in some abstract world of pure logic. At 11:00 a.m., one hour before my Linear Algebra class at noon, I decided that the air I breathed was more important than the Linear Algebra homework.*

*I went out on the grass, rolled and stretched myself out. I FELT FREE! I had "let go."*

Brian's journal [February 22, 1991]

### Meditations

*I started this week believing it would be mentally stressful because a philosophy paper and art project was due. On the contrary, this week has been physically stressful and mentally exploratory. While drawing a sketch of Buddha I spent a lot of time in meditation (often in a half-lotus), and a little time drawing Buddha in a full lotus posture. Thus the art work for philosophy was mentally relaxing.*

*Tuesday I did advance moves of the "co-bra" (in Yoga class) requiring good back flex-ibility. I did not do much beyond what I've done before, yet the next day my back was in great pain. Whenever I kept good back posture, and breathed abdominally with chest protruding, my back felt fine. If I slouched, or contracted my chest and back in the lung region, then I experi-enced pain in my mid-back. The pain did not let up until Friday evening while doing Ukemi (fall-ing technique) in Iaki Jujitsu.*

*Thursday at interpersonal group meeting George (the facilitator) suggested that for this coming week think about how my seizures are caused by my subconscious. He suggested that my seizures might be an "escape" from unbear-able conditions imposed by parents when I was a little boy. That whenever I could not deal with how everything in the family was, I would have a seizure to escape. I do not believe this is true, but I will think about it anyway (a little).*

*My eyes are getting sleepy. The clock says 11:40 p.m., so I am heading to bed. Maybe I will continue this writing tomorrow.*

Brian's Journal [March 1, 1991]

Unsurprisingly, the psychologist grasps for psychological causation of Brian's condition—just as John Menkes, the neurologist, had done years earlier. Brian isn't buying it. Of course the physiological domain and the psychological are not really separable. That's all the more reason not to focus narrowly on one causal explanation.

## *An Eventful Day*

*"Today has been quite eventful" were my first words in answer to the question, "How are you," when I went to a cafe this evening with Mike from interpersonal group. This morning I went and practiced "ukemi" with people from Daito Ryu club. I ate a healthy meal around four p.m.; spoke with Doug; finished designing "node structure" for CSC 450; I am twelve milligrams lower on my Tegretol dosage; yet I cannot attribute the "eventfulness" of today exactly to deeds done.*

*To keep brief, I attribute "eventfulness" to the breath with which I live life. Most influential is my practice of "shogyu" (hard work) with a few others from Daito Ryu. My overall feeling is one of comfort and satisfaction. There is no pain in my back, the "ukemi" (falling technique) removed all pain. As I reminisce about back pain I feel a little at this moment as I write. My mind has the power to create feelings of pain. As John said in class, perception of pain when sitting in "zazen" is all in the mind.*

*I also just finished a great or comfortable and interesting conversation with Mike, but I have little energy left to write since I must get up at 7:00 a.m. Our conversation focused on the expression of creative energy within, and Mike mentioned "kuadddim" which relates to the "kundalini yoga" I researched. I CANNOT—it seems—describe the "gist" of our conversation further. The clock says 11:10 p.m., so Good Night!*

Brian's journal [March 3, 1991]

About this time, Sue gave Brian a call. He was not at home, so she left a message for him to call back when he had a chance. We did not hear from him, but were not concerned. His priorities were now elsewhere. He'd get around to calling us sooner or later.

On March 3, there was the Rodney King beating in Los Angeles. We saw the tape, and were feeling somewhat sour about the police as a result.

On March 6, two policemen knocked on our door. I was working at home.

"There's been a terrible accident at Cal Poly in San Luis Obispo."

Brian had been found dead in his room in the afternoon. His roommate had been surprised that Brian was still in bed in the morning when he left for classes. When Brian was still in bed in the afternoon, he became concerned. Brian had had a seizure at about 1 a.m. the previous night. Two of his four roommates had heard it. However, this was not unprecedented, and therefore drew no further attention.

The mind revolts at the thought. I am like a fish at the end of a hook. Whenever the mind tries to go in one or another direction to find an escape from the truth that cannot be confronted, it is rudely jerked back. Again, and yet again.

Not Brian.

Not after all he has suffered.

Not after he is finally finding himself, and is starting to be happy.

Not now that he has finally found decent roommates.

Not now that he is a senior soon to graduate.

Not with all the life goals that he has set for himself.
Now it all becomes past tense.

One imagines what might have happened.
Was he perhaps aware of the fate that was befalling him?
Was he aware of his dilemma, but not in a position to save himself?

He had spoken so matter-of-factly of death. He considered it one option among many, and did not fear it. In his recent absorption with Eastern mysticism, death he learned was considered a mere transition.

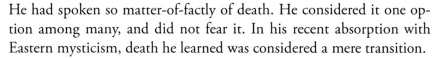

Sue came home an hour later from the clinic, and I had to tell her what happened. She took in the news with an incredible equanimity. I realized that what I had told her was just the culmination of fears that she had been carrying all along. She had already imagined a thousand deaths over the years. Here it finally actually happened. Sue knew well that with every grand mal seizure survival was in question.

We went to San Luis Obispo to meet with his roommates and with his professors. We met at the house of a faculty member in town. We all talked about the Brian that we had gotten to know. An article about Brian appeared in the *Mustang Daily*. Here finally was the obituary that his former roommate had joked about. His professor of Eastern Religions sent us Brian's drawing of the Buddha, marked with all the chakras. His math professor related some anecdotes, quirks of Brian's personality. The President of KME, the math honorary, invited me to give a talk about our work at the year-end graduation ceremony. We cleared out his room. We returned home with his ashes.

There was a memorial service for Brian at the Bel Air Presbyterian Church. Our friend, the Rev. Kent Smith of Los Gatos, presided. Brian's music teacher from High School, Eric Bluske, improvised on Brian's American Indian flute. Kurt's lower school teacher from Highland Hall, Bruce Laurelin, sang a song that he had written, which he accompanied with guitar. The organ music included the *Adagio* by Albeniz. Hearing it now becomes a different experience from what it was before. Several friends had written poems in memory of Brian. Several people connected with Highland Hall School read from Brian's journal. First there was Jim Storm, known to many for his acting on *The Young and the Restless*. There was Christine Lund, news anchor on Channel 4 in Los Angeles; and there was Dana Williams, one of Brian's favorite teachers from his High School years.

Hundreds of people had come, from the various threads of our lives. Many we had not seen for years. It was such a positive experience, but one that only such a tragedy could bring about. We spent the evening with close friends. The house was filled with flowers.

Then we were alone.

The following passage from Brian's journal was read at the memorial service by Christine Lund:

*I am sitting by a window seat on a jet plane flying home from Washington Dulles. Outside I see an ocean of clouds, turbid like white capped waves at sea. Now the clouds are quickly changing to soft rolling ridges, like rolling waves in the wake of a boat. The form is disappearing, becoming less well defined; the clouds appear like a white void, blank and monotonous as if you were inside the cloud. But I am above the clouds and I see blue sky far away. The blue sky is a thin line dividing an above larger cloud from the layers below me. Along the horizon the white clouds are bright, closer to me they look grey, for the sun lies low in the sky.*

*The veil of cloud above me looks like it is so near that climbing two flights of stairs might bring me to it. The veil is translucent with continuous fluctuation in opaqueness. Few areas are opaque enough that the blue sky cannot be seen through it.*

*Continually the cloud below me gains form and the blue sky is unveiled, and then the clouds lose form, becoming like a void as the blue sky is diminished to a faint line and then vanishes when the sky above appears opaque white as well.*

*The clouds I observe are a stratification of many layers. The clouds when close lie formless, but when far away the form of the cloud layer is revealed.*

*I am observing a thin veil below me. It looks different than the veil I saw above me because the light adds a different touch to the picture. Through the layer I see another cloud layer far below. Both layers have form.*

> *Now the fuzzy, opaque ocean of mist lies below me and only blue sky lies above.*
> Brian's journal [March 28, 1990]

## FOR BRIAN

Misty morning miracle...
A life that touches soul.
  Unique.
  Just once.
  A feather trace
That leaves an imprint fathoms deep
And so awakes the soul asleep.

Misty morning miracle...
A soul that touches life.
  At one.
  Within.
  Without; part of
Who joined his heart forever one,
And left the warming grace of sun.

Misty morning miracle...
A life that touched through life.
  Unique.
  Just once.
  A glowing gift,
Who lives forever in my soul
And joins me to the heart of whole.

Jane Gates, March 24, 1991

## REVERBERATIONS

The gift of Brian's journal disclosed dimensions of his mental struggle that he had not shared with us. He was now back home with us. We carry the burden of his memory. In our continuing work, we honor him. Brian had been a living presence with us for most of our adult lives. Going forward, his presence would be of a different kind. We are continuing to live with the person he was in 1991, not the 44-year-old he would be now. There is no basis for imagining such a person, but the son we lost remains a real presence in our lives even as our understanding of him continues to change.

In a significant way, Brian is now more vitally with us than when he was alive. I cannot say that he was daily in my thoughts when he was away at college. He was reasonably well-launched, and was largely making his own choices. But now he is ever-present. Perhaps this is something like the experience of phantom pain, where one feels the pain of a missing limb. The threads of connection to Brian have been severed, but they are all still alive and active. The engagement with our son continues.

Death does not mark life as a failure, even when it comes so early. The challenges Brian had to face caused him to live life intensely, and with awareness of its capriciousness and finitude. His willingness to face death with equanimity, expressed without reservation in his journal, testifies to a maturity uncommon for his years. In many respects, Brian's life was a triumph over the challenges he was given. He transcended the compartmentalization of our scientific models. He recognized that health involved more than neurology, and was ultimately a matter of the mind and of the spirit as well. Though scientifically inclined, he did not shrink from the implication that the very essence of our human experience is spiritual (though not, perhaps, in the traditional religious sense). He likewise did not shrink from investigating phenomena like telepathy, where most scientists have historically feared to tread. He simply went where the evidence and his experience took him.

We had benefited numerous times from Brian's counsel in our own EEG biofeedback work. We learned a lot from him about the complexities of right hemisphere training, and about hemispheric balance, and about global synchrony. We first experienced with him the benefit of inhibiting activity in the high beta (22-30 Hz) range. His software work on the Amiga had made our biofeedback instrument the most effective available. He could speak from personal experience to other people with a seizure disorder who were undergoing the training. An informal kind of partnership was emerging out of our mutual commitment to this field. All this would be painfully missed.

Early on I continued to imagine his continuing life journey in my mind. He might have worked on chaos theory, on how it applies to brain functioning, and to cortical stability. The combination of computer science with modeling of brain functioning interested him ("the science of complexity"). He might have become a professor in computer science. His math professor had said that Brian was his best student.

He might have helped bridge the gap between the different professional disciplines now addressing the problems of the brain: psychiatry, neurology, psychology, that are not presently communicating with each other.

He might have become a criminologist, with his insights into the problems of violence and aggressive behavior.

He might have brought some insight into the philosophical questions he raises with respect to mind-body dualism, our prevailing cultural bias.

These were all my dreams for Brian; they were not necessarily his own. I had not yet read his journal. What the journal makes plain most of all is the intimate entanglement of the life of the mind with the constraints of physiology. Time and again we see the flights of Brian's mind tethered to a squirrely and unreliable nervous system. How mightily he struggled to contain the volatility of his brain! I am in awe of the tenacity and determination Brian showed in containing his demons. He put his dreams of intimacy and relationship on hold pending the achievement of a reliable and stable brain. He could not drag others through his careening roller-coaster excursions between highs and lows. There is certain nobility of spirit here, hopeful and optimistic, punctuated at times by a confused and fragmented state of mind, steeped in the despair of self-loathing.

Brian's life exposed a central contradiction in our societies—the failure to acknowledge the degree to which our physiology constrains our life as moral agents—in addiction, in criminality, in PTSD, in minor head injury, in domestic violence, in sexual transgressions, in behavioral disorders, and just generally in our failure to live up to our highest and most humane aspirations. And now we have available the means to shed the constraints, to help us become more fully human. How much one wishes Brian could have witnessed the fruits of his own labors, and what his own suffering has inspired.

# 7

## PROGRESS AND RESISTANCE

Just as Brian had been moving from his own personal experience of neurofeedback to look-ing at its broader potential and his own possible contribution to the field, we were doing the same. With respect to developments in neuro-feedback, a whole new era was opening up for us that Brian could no longer be part of.

Just two weeks after Brian's death I was scheduled to give a talk at the national biofeedback conference in Houston, Texas on our just-completed study on neurofeedback in application to ADHD. I thought it so important for word to get out on our study that I dragged my limp and leaden limbs to the conference despite my state of psychic deple-tion. For the first time in my life, I was experiencing real physiological depression. I was moving through life as if wading through knee-deep water. Cognitive function suffered also. After the conference I shared a cab ride to Love Field, oblivious to the fact that my flight was booked out of Hobby airport.

The key finding of our study was an average increase in measured IQ score of about 23 points in our fifteen youngsters after their neurofeedback training, and other tests confirmed the changes. These were astounding findings, and they flew in the face of the strong belief at the time that IQ could not readily be altered. So matters could go one of two ways. Either the data would be accepted, which meant that the claims for neurofeedback had to be taken seriously, or the data would be rejected out of hand as being simply fanciful.

In this case, rejecting the data was not so easy because in fact we had not been the first to obtain such astounding results. We had been preceded by Michael Tansey, a clinical psychologist in private practice in New Jersey. He had obtained nominally 20-point IQ increases in a group of 24 mildly neurologically impaired children with his neurofeedback protocol, which differed just slightly from ours. He had to publish his results in a Canadian and an Australian journal because American journals would not countenance such claims. It was his study, published in 1990, that had prompted ours in the first place. We saw our work as a replication of his because our methods differed only in minor ways.

Since Tansey had already tilled the soil within the biofeedback community, so to speak, my report probably met with a better reception than it would have otherwise. A number of seasoned practitioners decided right then and there that they needed to make neurofeedback part of their skill set. The field as a whole, however, remained largely unmoved. After all, the history of the field was populated with extraordinary claims, and that had never gone well before. Besides, it takes more than one tugboat to redirect an ocean liner.

Is it realistic to expect such huge changes in IQ score with nothing more than a few neurofeedback training sessions (about 20 to 60)? For appropriate candidates, the answer is yes. These middle school and high school children were not functioning at their apparent potential for one reason or another, and most of them had behavioral problems—some of them quite severe. Most of them also had sleep issues, and for a large minority head pain and stomach pain was commonplace. The training had helped them across the board, in all of their areas of dysfunction.

The tests were selected to emphasize the improvements in cognitive function. That was for two principal reasons. First of all, these are most readily quantifiable, and we needed numbers to have an impact. But more fundamentally, in addressing ADHD we were operating within the prevailing models of cognitive neuroscience. We were narrowly focused on left hemisphere function, on what is called executive function, and on the failures of directed attention. Appropriately, it was largely the left hemisphere that was being trained.

The clinical psychologist who had done the pre-post testing for us, Clifford Marks, had a very different impression of the whole experience. He was blown away by the changes.

"These children are different," he said. "This is so easy!"

How would he know, I thought to myself. He hadn't been involved in the training process at all. After all, the whole point was that he would be an independent tester who was not already invested in the procedure. He explained what he meant. "We work for years with kids like this and don't expect to get changes like these."

The testing experience sometimes differed like day and night. Those who had been surly, uncooperative, and devil-may-care children in the pre-test were now engaged and eager to perform. So the change in scores didn't reflect purely gains in intellectual capacity, although that had to be the bulk of it. The lack of engagement may help to explain some of the poor initial scores, but good intentions don't explain the superb final scores. The average final IQ score was 130! We had gone way beyond remediating deficits. We were improving function well beyond age-appropriate average performance.

The kids also showed vastly improved short-term memory. A number of them jumped several grade levels in reading and/or arithmetic achievement. And several even changed handedness, along with a general improvement in manual dexterity. That does not come from good intentions, and it cannot be explained in terms of any "placebo" model, the favorite cudgel with which critics flog any new therapeutic procedure.

But the bigger story lay beyond the numbers, as Clifford Marks had recognized. These children were now different, and the trajectory of their lives would surely now be better in consequence. These children had been affected in their emotional being, and that had a favorable impact on their relationships with family members, friends, and teachers. They now ran with a more even keel. And they now had better command of their inherent intellectual gifts.

## Rejection

The problem we faced was that there was no way to communicate this larger perspective to the scientific and professional community. We were dealing with "soft" data, observations that are not readily quantifiable. But it was worse than that. The entire realm of the emotions had been set aside by the scientists involved with ADHD. That wasn't going to change until the 21st century. This can be explained by the observation that there is typically a payoff for narrow focus in scientific research. Generalists need not apply. In the research community, some issues are attended to with perseverative zeal, whereas other issues are off the table.

A second characteristic of such scientific communities is that they mount an active defense against propositions that don't conform to the prevailing paradigm. The very notion of improving IQ was so preposterous that it served to discredit neurofeedback all by itself. The force of established authority twisted the best evidence in our favor into the strongest evidence against us. We were obviously not operating on a level playing field. We had encountered a bizarre world.

Gradually taking shape in our minds was the view that the neurofeedback was affecting a variety of brain functions, just as had been the case with Brian. That notion was already familiar from traditional biofeedback, where a few basic methods would be drawn upon to address a wide range of conditions, from anxiety to panic disorder, from migraine to asthma, and from muscle tension headaches to TMJ. Neurofeedback had started out looking very different, targeting seizure disorder specifically. But already there were indications of sleep being favorably impacted, as well as the disparate symptoms associated with ADHD.

Margaret Ayers, meanwhile, extrapolated from the seizure work to traumatic brain injury in general, including stroke. All the common symptoms of traumatic brain injury responded to one degree or another to the training: headache, nausea, vertigo, mental confusion, effort fatigue, loss of cognitive function, lack of planning ability, pain syndromes, sleep irregularities, emotional disregulation, etc. Just because we were all training the brain with a very narrowly targeted method did not mean that the results were narrowly specific. Margaret had been the first to realize the breadth of the potential of neurofeedback. In the case of traumatic brain injury and stroke rehabilitation she faced no push-back because the medical community as a whole was just not very interested in the problem.

Still, the scientific world required definitive evidence for very specific claims in order to move the agenda. This was going to be particularly tough when the topic under discussion was ADHD, which is inherently a broadly inclusive, rather mushy concept. We had to operate on two levels. In our work we continued to elaborate a model based on neurofeedback resolving core issues of disregulation, while in our interaction with the professions we continued to speak narrowly to what was acceptable. The key goal remained that of making inroads into the established professions to gain a hearing for neurofeedback. The most promising avenue was to continue the push with ADHD, as there was already some support in the literature for this application.

## Media Attention

By 1993 we had attracted some attention in Los Angeles with our work, and we were invited to demonstrate neurofeedback on ABC's *The Home Show*. This introduced us to the magical world of Hollywood. The producers wanted a live demonstration with a young trainee, and in order to keep the child from wilting under the glare of cameras, etc., an entire clinic room was constructed on the set to allow for hidden cameras.

The show was scheduled for 6:00 a.m., in time for a 9:00 a.m. live showing on the East Coast. When the cameras were just about to go live, the lights suddenly went out in our little clinic room. That's all we needed, as the two of us in the room were already tense and on high alert. I had rehearsed some possible opening commentary, and now all of that was out the window. But matters were quickly rescued. The demonstration went well, and I explained to the audience that the girl was making Pac-Man (the Mazes game) go with her brain. Gary Collins and Sarah Purcell, co-hosts of the show, seemed impressed but slightly wary. Their medical consultant, pediatrician Jay Gordon, was surprisingly supportive. "I'm trying very hard to be skeptical," he said. That is the default position for an MD confronted with novelty. But he was not succeeding. This was just biofeedback, after all, which had long been accepted within medicine. "I wish they would publish some studies in recognized journals so I wouldn't have to argue with my colleagues about this." Gordon's nod toward neurofeedback had been totally unexpected, but very welcome.

The show had an incredible impact that brought home to us the urgency of what we were doing. Sue was at home recovering from surgery at the time of the production, but even while the show was still on the air she started receiving calls from the East Coast. Calls had been forwarded to our home from the office. We had over 140 pieces of mail the very next day, one of them post-marked as far away as Indiana. We received over 5,000 inquiries overall within a matter of days. The stories told in these letters were often heart-rending. People got it. This was not just about ADHD. We got inquiries about cerebral palsy and many other conditions. The world was ready for neurofeedback. We have held onto all of this correspondence over the years. I was never able to let it go.

## Ramping Up

At this time there were no more than a hundred or so neurofeedback practitioners around the country who could step in to help these people, and we got in touch with them for the referrals. Alas, most of them would not accept any condition that was not standard-issue ADHD. We had created this demand for neurofeedback without any way of meeting it. We ramped up our professional training schedule to six training courses within the year.

In 1993 a new conference was organized with EEG biofeedback as the theme. It took place in Key West, Florida. It was at this conference that we first decided to "go public" with the more inclusive view of neurofeedback, one that went beyond seizures and ADHD to encompass a wide range of ailments. There was hostility to this view from those who were more focused on ADHD, including in particular Joel Lubar. The formal argument that ensued was of course about the sufficiency of the evidence we had for our numerous propositions. But the real issue went well beyond the facts. It was a question of tactics.

Lubar saw it as much more strategic to make the case for one condition, such as ADHD, than to take on the whole frontier of mental health. He was personally committed to that more strategic path. He thought that our making the larger case was sending a mixed message, which made his task much more difficult. We, on the other hand, had just come from the exhilarating experience of being on The Home Show, and saw a huge unmet need for which neurofeedback was the obvious remedy.

The very next month, in March of 1993, a new professional organization formed around neurofeedback (The Society for the Study of Neuronal Regulation, the SSNR), and had its organizational meeting on Catalina Island. The impetus had been provided by our own clinical office. One of the three organizers of the SSNR, Ken Tachiki, had just visited our office, and he grasped the potential immediately. Tachiki was another researcher at the Sepulveda Veterans Administration Hospital where neurofeedback had been birthed.

With those three events in such close proximity, we had the growing sense that momentum was building behind neurofeedback and that the world of mental health might soon be transformed. My expectations were no doubt affected by the pace of change I was used to in the technological sector, where I had spent twenty years. But healthcare is different. It is not enough to convince the client. To really effect change, one has to bring the whole professional community on board.

### Large-Scale Controlled Study

In order to bring that about, we decided to sponsor a large-scale controlled study of neurofeedback for ADHD in 1993-4. The study was to be designed and conducted by university-based researchers. Our role would be just to do the neurofeedback training. Testing and evaluation would be entirely the burden of the researchers. There were three groups: an EEG training group, a wait-list group, and a cognitive skills training group. The wait-list group got neurofeedback later. Initial results of the study were presented as a poster paper at the Annual Meeting of the American Psychological Association, which took place at the Biltmore Hotel in Los Angeles in 1994. I remember the event well, because my car, a 1969 BMW 2800, had its windows smashed in the public parking lot for at most a few coins that I might have left in the car. But that wasn't the bad news.

Professor Russell Barkley, Director of Psychology at the University of Massachusetts, and a vocal critic of EEG biofeedback for ADHD, ripped the findings in his next issue of his ADHD Report. He had in fact been given cause. The authors took care not to stir the waters any more than necessary, so they took the most conservative view of the data that could reasonably be taken.

Missing from the report was the essential data point that we had been working with children who were largely (85%) already medicated, and some (15%) were even on multiple medications. This happened because the main referral source for the study was pediatricians. So we were in effect testing for the additive effect of neurofeedback beyond what was achievable with medications. At the same time these pediatricians were not conversant with neurofeedback, and weren't prepared to decrease the medications when that was indicated. So some kids ended up over-medicated.

Despite all this, the study had found a highly significant improvement in the hyperactivity scale—with a population already medicated for hyperactivity! That should have been the signal finding to come out of that study. Instead we heard about all the tests that did not show significant improvement. Most of these tests had been put into the mix for the benefit of the cognitive skills training arm. They were not so relevant to ADHD.

Once again we found our own data being twisted around to be used against the claim we were hoping to prove, just as happened in the case of the IQ data. We were being beaten up with our own data—with the study that we had paid for dearly. All of the training had been given at no charge. This tied up our Pasadena office for the better part of a year. We also had to pay Cal Poly for their involvement.

There were further consequences. Quite possibly because the researchers were intimidated by the hostility of Russell Barkley, the research findings were never published, so the partial analysis from the poster paper is all that we have for our efforts. I found this quite unbelievable as it transpired, but this was apparently how the world works that we now had to navigate through. The real world was that of politics around professional issues; the science was mere window-dressing.

In 1996 Dennis Cantwell came to visit our office in Encino. Cantwell held the Joseph Campbell Chair in Child Psychiatry at the UCLA Neuropsychiatric Institute, and was a renowned authority on ADHD. Not a year before he had still been pounding the lectern with denunciations of the claims for neurofeedback, and yet here he was. The impetus was the finding that children on Ritalin, and on combinations of Ritalin and Clonidine, would in rare cases suffer sudden cardiac death. In these cases there would be no warning. In an autopsy on one such child, who had been on Ritalin a mere six months, the MD found himself looking at 'a cocaine heart,' what he expected to see in a long-term coaine user. "ADHD may be a terrible thing," said Cantwell, "but it doesn't kill you, and neither should the remedy. So if there was anything at all to this new therapy, we really need to know."

We agreed on a study format in which we would do all of the training and he would do all of the assessments. A proposal along those lines received UCLA Human Subjects clearance and was ready to be submitted to the NIMH.

It was April 14, 1997 when UCLA Professor Allan Schore came to visit with two of his colleagues. As Sue and I were telling them excitedly about the research design we were interrupted by one of the guests. "Apparently you don't yet know that Dennis Cantwell died last night." Cantwell was not yet 59.

We met with the new head of Child Psychiatry, James McCracken, who wanted to keep the project going. "We consider it to be part of Dennis' legacy." But it didn't happen. The person he assigned to the task, James McGough, was unenthusiastic. We would have to continue to toil on our own. The death risk of children on stimulant medication presumably remains.

### Addictions Treatment

In 1995 we had an opportunity to launch a research project on neurofeedback in support of addictions treatment. This would focus on the other main thrust in neurofeedback, the alpha-theta training that grew out of the work of Joe Kamiya, the original discoverer of EEG biofeedback. We had been so impressed with the results of a research study performed by Eugene Peniston with veteran alcoholics at the Fort Lyon VA Medical Center in Colorado. Peniston had spent years there as a psychologist working with war-related alcoholism, and the results had been abysmal until he introduced neurofeedback. In 1992 he presented results of a three-year follow-up, in which he reported that abstinence was being sustained. Peniston had found a remedy for PTSD, effectively, and for the substance dependency that often went along with it.

Our opportunity came with the willingness of a local residential treatment center, CRI Help, to sponsor the research and to fund the effort. Our role would be limited to training their staff to conduct the training, to supervise the actual training, and to furnish the instrumentation. We also designed the whole study, but the organization took charge of all the testing and follow-up. A matched control group would just get the normal services offered by this treatment center, and the experimental subjects would get the neurofeedback training in addition. All the testing was to be done in a blinded fashion, in which the testers did not know to which group the testee belonged.

The outcomes were impressive. First, the experimentals stayed in the program twice as long as the controls. That's good news, because outcome improves with length of stay. Second, there was considerable improvement in attentional scores among the experimentals, versus no significant change among the controls. Third, there were major changes in personality variables compared to far fewer among the controls. And finally the experimentals performed three times better than controls when it came to abstinence one year after release from the program. After three years, the experimentals were largely holding their gains, whereas the controls had suffered further attrition.

The results were first presented at the Annual Meeting of the American Association for the Advancement of Science in 1999, but the results were not published until 2005, after four failed attempts at getting the paper accepted. From that time forward, neurofeedback has been among the services offered at CRI Help, but the training has only been offered selectively. Only certain categories qualified for the training (such as ADHD, for example), which meant that CRI Help management did not come to see neurofeedback as a primary treatment for addictions. They held onto the belief on which the CRI Help program was originally founded, namely that addiction is at root a problem of personal failure. Their emphasis remained on psychotherapeutic techniques in the context of a 12-step program.

## *Bipolar Disorder*

1995 was noteworthy for one other significant development in our neurofeedback work. We reported success in working with Bipolar Disorder. We had seen only a few cases, but the condition is so intractable clinically that any success at all needed to be shared with the growing neurofeedback professional community. Our clinical success had been stunning indeed. A woman came to see us who had been told by her psychiatrist that since she could not tolerate any of the medications the only option left was ECT, electroconvulsive shock therapy. This did not frighten her, but she was concerned about the anesthesia she would have to undergo for the procedure, in view of her medication intolerance. She heard about our work and wanted to try neurofeedback before taking on the risk of the anesthesia.

Her condition was stabilized over a good many sessions. After a year, she went back to see her psychiatrist. He was stunned.

"You look like a different person," he said, as tears welled up in his eyes. "I have worried more about you than about anyone else in my practice." Those about whom he had been comparably worried in the past were no longer among the living. Bipolar Disorder is associated with a large suicide risk, and it had been very much an issue in this case. Over the course of training, this risk had been markedly moderated, to the point where it was no longer a concern.

Our report received a mixed reception at the conferences—a bipolar reception, one might say. Either the results implied far more therapeutic potency for neurofeedback than anyone suspected, or the whole report should just be dismissed out of hand because there simply had to be another explanation. There was also familiar element in play. Bipolar Disorder was seen as a mental disorder rather than as a physiological one. This was about anxiety and depression, core concerns of psychotherapists. Seizure disorder belonged in the neurology camp, and did not threaten the field of psychology. Attention Deficit Disorder was being framed as a neurobiological condition. But Bipolar Disorder? That was psychology in its essence. With our new claims we were challenging psychology. It has been seventeen years since, and over most of that time Bipolar Disorder has remained ring-fenced within the neurofeedback field; it is rarely talked about.

## *Training Abroad*

1995 was also the year when we took our professional training course abroad. We conducted our first training courses in Sydney, Australia, and in Munich, Germany. We were invited by the Department of Neurology at Charles University in Prague to lecture there for a day. We had brought Barry Sterman with us, as he was then a member of our teaching staff. The Czech Republic was only six years from the time the Iron Curtain had been lifted. One of the attending neurologists had remembered Sterman's earlier work, so he was eager to be updated.

The assembly thought they were getting the latest and the best out of the United States. Indeed they were, but we also had to tell them that this was not yet clear to people in the United States. After our presentation, the Department of Neurology promptly decided to include neurofeedback in their academic program, and neurofeedback started flourishing in the Czech Republic as nowhere else in the world. Within just a few years there sprouted hundreds of neurofeedback practitioners in that small country.

# 8
# DEVELOPMENT
# OF THE OTHMER
# METHOD

1995 was the last year in which we used largely the standard methods that had been handed down to us from Sterman, Ayers, Lubar, Tansey, Kamiya and Peniston. This was the first time we deviated from the standard frequencies that had been handed down to us as well. From that time forward, we increasingly relied on personalization of the training parameters, and that opened the door to the evolution of the method in ways that eventually bore little resemblance to our starting point. In retrospect, that all seems straightforward enough. But at the time these incremental migrations away from the standard approaches seemed daring because they meant the abandonment of the models that we had in our heads. We went from the sensorimotor rhythm being something very special to where we realized that training could usefully be done at any EEG frequency and at any point on the scalp. One just had to figure out the applicable rules. That process, however, took many years.

It was the procedure of incremental adjustment that eventually led us to explore the entire EEG spectrum to find whatever the client responded to best. It was by means of individualization of the training that our clinical reach continued to increase over a wider range of clinical conditions. Since people were largely coming to us as a last resort, we were succeeding with a wide variety of cases regarded as medically intractable, and with conditions regarded as relatively untreatable.

As if by gravity, we tended to be pulled more and more toward the lower EEG frequencies as the most effective. This opened up for us greater training opportunities on the right hemisphere, where our primary emotions are principally organized. The most intractable conditions, we found out, tended to be those that were intimately connected with emotional disregulation. Typically these emotional deficits were traceable to adverse early childhood events or life experience. These adverse events might be physical in nature (birth injury, high fevers, or mild head injury) or of psychological import (family break-up, parental drug use or other mental health issue, adoption).

We were effectively compensating for earlier developmental deficits. We were helping the brain to better function, in consequence of which the dysfunctions would subside. The right hemisphere was the key to the emotional realm, whereas the field as a whole had largely been preoccupied with the left hemisphere. We had found early on that the right hemisphere optimized differently from the left. It always optimized at lower frequencies than the left, and always in a simple mathematical relationship that held true all across the spectrum.

It was in 2005 that Sue was invited to present the evolution of her clinical approach of personalized neurofeedback at the annual conference of the ISNR, the International Society for Neuronal Regulation, successor to the SSNR. A rather complete story could be told of our systematic development of the individualized approach to EEG training that by this time covered the entire range of the EEG, down to as low as one could go with standard methods. Unbeknownst to us at the time, that recapitulation of our development path also represented the end of one era, and the beginning of another. Right after that meeting, it turns out, the journey took us to a new way of doing neurofeedback.

This departure upset so many of the standard assumptions we all had been making about neurofeedback that controversy was inevitable. That controversy persists to this day, some seven years later. Since we were relatively alone in pursuing this path, it is being referred to as The Othmer Method.

## *Migration to Lower Frequencies*

The last seven years have seen a steady progression of our work down to ever lower frequencies, frequencies much lower than what was being routinely measured in the EEG. Unconventional hardware and software needed to be devised to do this. But otherwise the approach remained the same. It just became clear that the brain related more readily to this very low-frequency information, and our clinical results reflected this.

Fortuitously, we were getting help from the neurosciences, where the latest imaging techniques were also engaged with brain behavior at these very low frequencies. This imaging work revealed the existence of core networks that organize the neuronal conversation. Here we found the answer to our puzzle of why these low frequencies were so useful. When the brain is given information on the activity of those core networks, it finds that information helpful in the recovery of function. This is self-healing at a very fundamental level. We had found a way to train these network relations simply by feeding the relevant information back to the brain.

The whole process is largely directed by the brain itself. Our role is merely to shine a light on the relevant activity, and to allow the process to unfold. Beyond that, it is to guide it to its best outcome on the basis of the results that we see. We are training brain function at its most foundational, namely the capacity of the brain to regulate itself. We judge our outcome by the subsidence of dysfunction.

## *Brian's Legacy*

When Brian began training his brain in 1985, Margaret Ayers was using essentially one protocol, and we picked up that theme when we began our work. As soon as protocol choices opened up for us just a few years later it became necessary to devise schema for decision-making. And when we made the reward frequency continuously adjustable it became necessary to also adopt an optimization procedure. From that time on, the individualization of the training became the driver of innovation.

It is always the most difficult cases that are most in need of the individualization of training, and over time these drove us to ever lower frequencies, as well as to an ever greater preoccupation with the right hemisphere. A pattern began to be observed that the most challenging cases tended to involve emotional regulation, and they typically were associated with issues traceable back to early childhood. This had also been Brian's story, once we had the perspective to view it in this fashion.

So what the low-frequency training has given us, in addition to everything else, is access to injury done in early childhood, provided that it lies in the functional realm. Such lingering deficits can be seen as the downside of brain plasticity, and now we are drawing on that same brain plasticity to effect recovery. This has given us a remedy for rather intractable conditions such as Conduct Disorder, Reactive Attachment Disorder, the autistic spectrum, addiction, and the personality disorders.

The over-arching issue is Developmental Trauma, which has emerged as a key concern in a large fraction of our clinical population. Whenever this is indicated in a client history it determines the training approach. It trumps all other clinical concerns. None of this was known over the years that Brian was able to do neurofeedback. And yet it was Sue's life with Brian that set us on this path, and it was our experience with Brian's training that has informed our work ever since. Brian's life has been our lodestar, and it has given our mission urgency.

THIS IS Brian's LEGACY...

# ACKNOWLEDGMENTS

Sue Othmer was the primary influence on Brian throughout his life. Typically a mother feels the greater burden of getting children well launched, and that was the case in our household as well. It was my impulse originally to tell the story. And whereas this book is Brian's story—and mine, it is Sue's as well. Brian continued neurofeedback training with Sue as we developed our new instrumentation. Sue was responsible for the evolution of our neurofeedback methods over the years, and her work shaped instrumentation development to its present mature state. Sue has taught professionals how to do neurofeedback since 1990. Sue's clinical approach is now being used by thousands of clinicians in over fifty countries, and it has influenced developments throughout the field. By now between one and two million people have experienced neurofeedback according to methods developed by Sue Othmer.

Our son Kurt also played a key role in Brian's life, much more than is apparent in the book, particularly in the years after Brian started the neurofeedback. Fortunately he was also swept up in the excitement of the neurofeedback frontier, and decided after college to enter the field as well. With degrees in psychology and economics, he has been in charge of our business since 2002, and that has allowed me to take the time to complete this book.

Brian's venture into neurofeedback would not have occurred had it not been for our friend since graduate school, Sue Rosen. She happened upon neurofeedback while seeking help for her own autistic daughter Sarah. Our families have an extended shared history of raising neurologically challenged children. Sue Rosen opened our first neurofeedback clinical practice in San Francisco, one week prior to the opening of our own office in Los Angeles in the late fall of 1988.

The text has not reflected the important role played throughout by Edward Dillingham, our software writer for the NeuroCybernetics system. It took a good deal of faith and courage for Ed to undertake the software writing task for a number of years without income, and before we really knew the larger potential of the method. We are so grateful. This leads me to acknowledge the role of his wife, Jean Dillingham, who supported Ed through all the highs and lows of our adventure. The highs were mostly ethereal; the lows were mostly very real.

Our venture into the current era of neurofeedback was made possible by Bernhard Wandernoth. Bernhard is a German engineer working in Switzerland. Among other accomplishments, he developed the state-of-the-art satellite laser communications system for the European Space Agency. He was motivated to investigate neurofeedback for his own son's needs in 2004, when we met at a conference in Winterthur, Switzerland. He said to himself at the time: "Even if only 10% of what Siegfried says about neurofeedback actually holds up, that is enough to justify my getting involved."

He offered his services to design modern instrumentation, and our current Cygnet system emerged out of that enduring partnership. Cygnet is the term for a baby swan—a name that suggests growth, promise and potential. It is also the name of a small lake in the Swan Valley in Montana where we had spent many a vacation.

I also want to acknowledge the help of a number of people with the editing of the book. First I want to thank Pam Tarr for helping to shape the book at the outset, and then for taking the initial cut of the scythe on the manuscript to trim it down to its current size. David Wisehart arranged Brian's journal by topics and edited the text. Deena Metzger reviewed the manuscript and made helpful suggestions.

Also standing behind the book is our wonderful staff at EEG Info and the EEG Institute. I also want to acknowledge those who worked with us for many years with our first venture, EEG Spectrum.

Beyond this, there are all the people who came to our professional training courses over the years and took up this work. At the outset that was quite a gamble, and we appreciate all of the early adopters who took that chance.

The whole edifice rests ultimately on all our clients over the last 25 years, who heard us and took a chance on neurofeedback. They trusted us with their brains, often against the advice of friends, family, and health professionals. Nearly everything we now know about neurofeedback we have learned from our clients.

# ABOUT THE AUTHOR

Since 1985 Siegfried Othmer has been engaged in the development of research-grade instrumentation for EEG feedback, and since 1987 has been involved in the research of clinical applications utilizing that instrumentation. Currently he is Chief Scientist at the EEG Institute in Woodland Hills, CA.

From 1987–2000 he was President of EEG Spectrum, and until 2002 served as Chief Scientist of EEG Spectrum Inter-national. Dr. Othmer provides training for professionals in EEG biofeedback, and presents research findings in professional forums.

Dr. Othmer has been President of the Neurofeedback Division of the Association for Applied Psychophysiology and Biofeedback for the past two years (2011-2013).

CPSIA information can be obtained at www.ICGtesting.com
Printed in the USA
BVOW011921110713

325735BV00003B/7/P